SO-AHT-432

GREEN LANTERN
NEW GUARDIANS

VOLUME 4 **GODS AND MONSTERS**

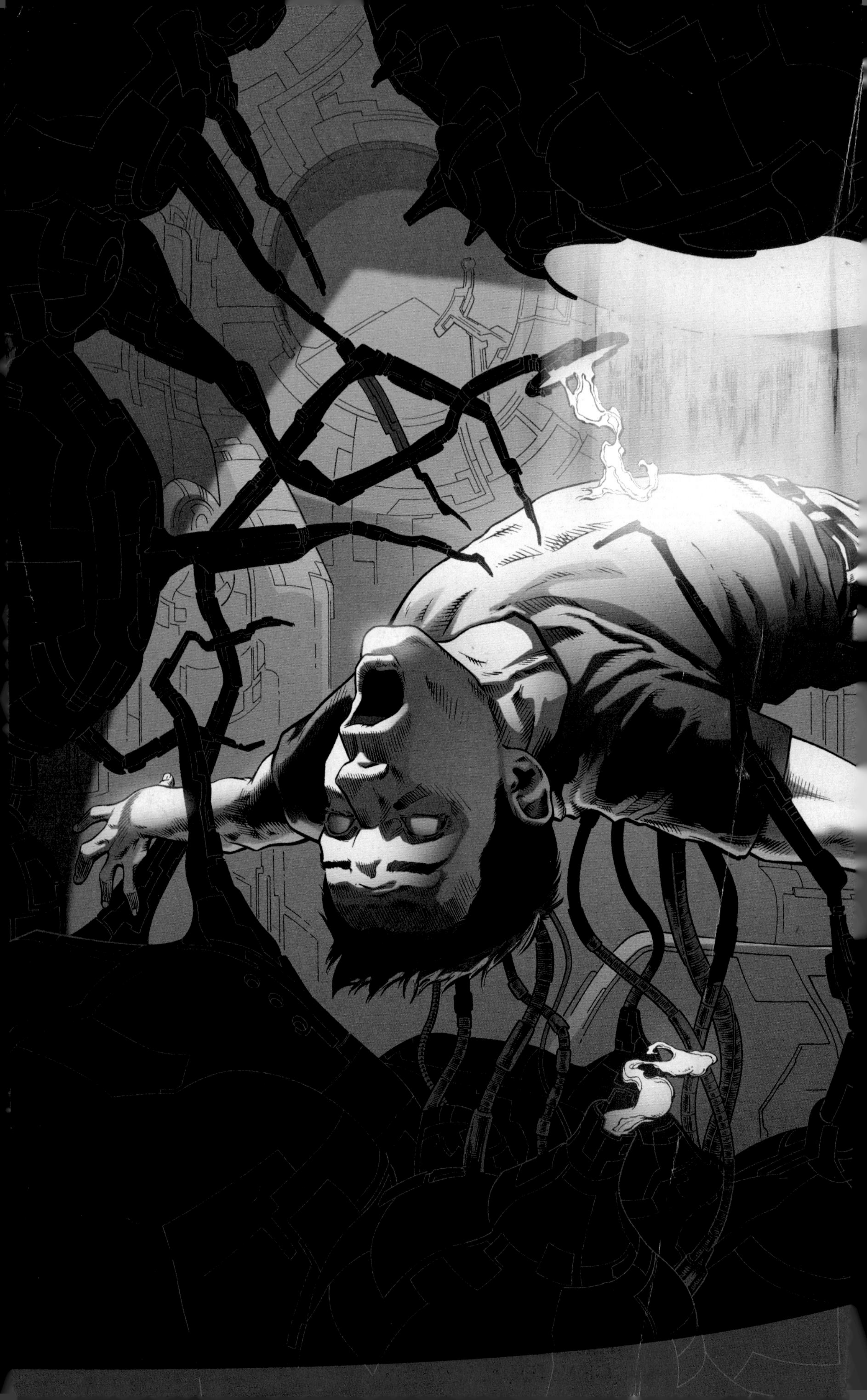

GREEN LANTERN
NEW GUARDIANS

VOLUME 4
GODS AND MONSTERS

JUSTIN **JORDAN**
ROBERT VENDITTI writers

BRAD **WALKER** GERALDO **BORGES**
ANDREI **BRESSAN** SEAN **CHEN** pencillers

ANDREW **HENNESSY** ANDREI **BRESSAN**
MARIAH **BENES** MARC **DEERING** J.P. **MAYER**
JON **SIBAL** CAM **SMITH** RYAN **WINN** WALDEN **WONG** inkers

WIL **QUINTANA** **HI-FI** ANDREW **DALHOUSE** colorists

CARLOS M. **MANGUAL** DEZI **SIENTY** DAVE **SHARPE** letterers

BRAD **WALKER**, ANDREW **HENNESSY** & WIL **QUINTANA**
collection cover artists

CHRIS CONROY Editor – Original Series RACHEL PINNELAS Editor
ROBBIN BROSTERMAN Design Director – Books ROBBIE BIEDERMAN Publication Design

BOB HARRAS Senior VP – Editor-in-Chief, DC Comics

DIANE NELSON President DAN DIDIO and JIM LEE Co-Publishers GEOFF JOHNS Chief Creative Officer
AMIT DESAI Senior VP – Marketing and Franchise Management
AMY GENKINS Senior VP – Business and Legal Affairs NAIRI GARDINER Senior VP – Finance
JEFF BOISON VP – Publishing Planning MARK CHIARELLO VP – Art Direction and Design
JOHN CUNNINGHAM VP – Marketing TERRI CUNNINGHAM VP – Editorial Administration
LARRY GANEM VP – Talent Relations and Services ALISON GILL Senior VP – Manufacturing and Operations
HANK KANALZ Senior VP – Vertigo and Integrated Publishing JAY KOGAN VP – Business and Legal Affairs, Publishing
JACK MAHAN VP – Business Affairs, Talent NICK NAPOLITANO VP – Manufacturing Administration SUE POHJA VP – Book Sales
FRED RUIZ VP – Manufacturing Operations COURTNEY SIMMONS Senior VP – Publicity BOB WAYNE Senior VP – Sales

GREEN LANTERN: NEW GUARDIANS: VOLUME 4: GODS AND MONSTERS

DC Comics, 1700 Broadway, New York, NY 10019
A Warner Bros. Entertainment Company.
Printed by RR Donnelley, Salem, VA, USA. 7/25/14. First Printing.

ISBN: 978-1-4012-4746-1

SUSTAINABLE FORESTRY INITIATIVE

Certified Chain of Custody
20% Certified Forest Content,
80% Certified Sourcing
www.sfiprogram.org
SFI-01042
APPLIES TO TEXT STOCK ONLY

Library of Congress Cataloging-in-Publication Data
Library of Congress Cataloging-in-Publication Data

Jordan, Justin, author.
Green Lantern: New Guardians. Volume 4, Gods and Monsters / Justin Jordan, Brad Walker.
pages cm — (The New 52!)
ISBN 978-1-4012-4746-1 (paperback)
1. Graphic novels. I. Walker, Brad (Comic book artist) illustrator. II. Title. III. Title: Gods and Monsters.
PN6728.G74J69 2014
741.5'973—dc23
2014011631

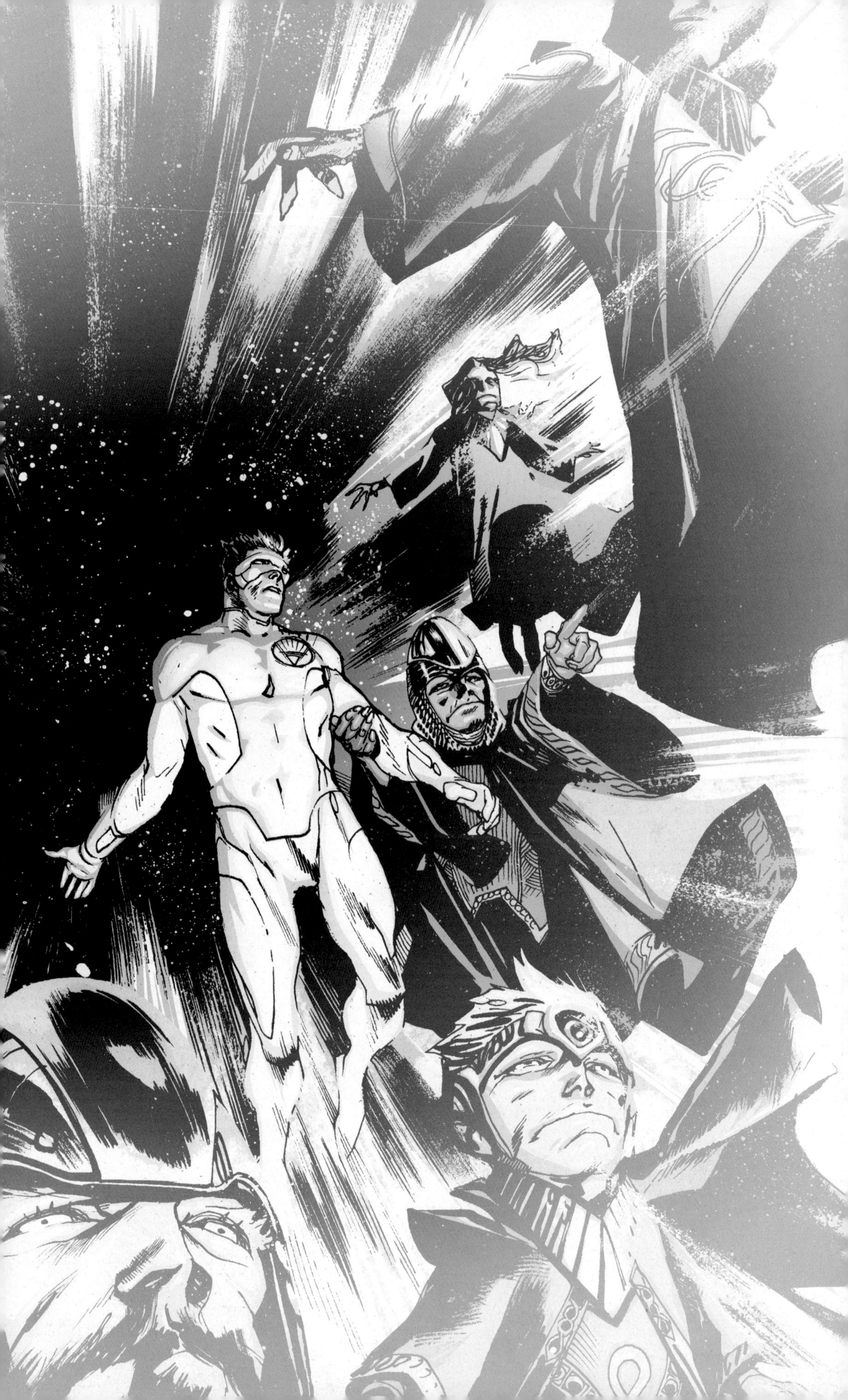

THE ANOMALY
JUSTIN JORDAN writer BRAD WALKER penciller ANDREW HENNESSY inker
cover art by RAFAEL ALBUQUERQUE & DAVE McCAIG RELIC variant cover by RAGS MORALES

"THE OLD GUARDIANS *FAILED.*

"*WORSE* THAN FAILED... THEY BETRAYED EVERYTHING WE ONCE BELIEVED. AND FOR THAT THEY HAVE BEEN *PUNISHED.* DAMNED AND DESTROYED.

"BUT WE ARE NOT THEM.

"THIS HORROR WILL NOT HAPPEN AGAIN. WHICH IS WHY WE ARE PROPOSING TO *LEAVE* THIS PLACE. TO LEAVE OA."

OUR BROTHERS AND SISTERS BELIEVED THAT THEY COULD POLICE THIS UNIVERSE *WITH-OUT* BEING A PART OF IT. AND BECAUSE THEY CLOSED THEMSELVES OFF FROM ALL THAT WAS OUTSIDE, ALL THEY HEARD WAS THEIR OWN EGO.

THIS UNIVERSE IS FULL OF WONDERS. WE HAVE ALREADY SPENT FAR TOO LONG AWAY. SO WE WILL *SEE* IT, THE HORRORS AND THE GLORY. WE WILL BE *IN* IT, SO THAT WE DO NOT MAKE THE SAME MISTAKES.

YOU WILL BE OUR GUIDE AND GUARDIAN. YOU WILL SHOW US WHAT IT IS TO BE PART OF THE GRAND COMMUNITY. YOU WILL SEE THINGS NO MAN HAS DREAMED OF.

THIS IS WHAT WE ASK OF YOU, *KYLE RAYNER.*

NO.

I... EXCUSE ME?

SORRY, LET ME BE MORE CLEAR.

HELL NO.

...CUTE.

BUT I THINK THE GREEN IS SENDING A MIXED MESSAGE, HAL. I'M FEELING SOMETHING ELSE ENTIRELY.

SORRY... NOT *ALL* OF US CAN PAINT WITH EVERY COLOR IN THE SPECTRUM.

I HOPE YOU'RE NOT HERE TO TRY TO MAKE ME TAKE THE *SMURFS* ON SAFARI...

MAKE? I'M NOT SURE I COULD. AND FRANKLY, I'M TIRED OF FIGHTING. I'M ESPECIALLY TIRED OF FIGHTING PEOPLE WHO SHOULD BE ON MY SIDE.

SO I THOUGHT I'D TRY SOMETHING NOVEL.

I THOUGHT I'D *ASK.*

I APPRECIATE IT. BUT THE ANSWER IS STILL NO. AND I HAVE THINGS TO DO.

LIKE WHAT?

NOW? RIGHT NOW I NEED TO FIND SOMETHING TO *HIT.*

I DIDN'T EVEN KNOW THERE *WAS* SUCH A THING AS A "SPACE SHARK"...

THIS'LL DO.

THERE ARE, BUT THESE...SOMEONE HAS *DONE* SOMETHING TO THEM. THEY DON'T NORMALLY ATTACK GIL'DISHPAN SPACESHIPS FOR THE HECK OF IT.

WHICH IS *ONE* OF THE REASONS WHY I'M NOT GOING TO BABYSIT THE GUARDIANS. WE'VE SPENT SO MUCH TIME SORTING OUT THE PROBLEMS THAT THEY CREATED, AND FIGHTING EACH OTHER...

...MEANWHILE, OUT IN THE UNIVERSE, THERE ARE MAD SCIENTISTS AND ALIEN CONQUERORS SHARPENING THEIR SWORDS.

YOU SPEND TOO MUCH TIME ON *ONE* THREAT...

UH, KYLE...?

...YOU DON'T SEE THE BIGGER ONES CREEPING UP BEHIND YOU.

OF COURSE, SOMETIMES YOU *DO.*

YOU'RE CHANNELING RED?

YEAH. SO YOU CAN IMAGINE MY MOOD.

I DIDN'T THINK YOU COULD DO THAT--USE THE RING TO *INFECT* THEM WITH RAGE.

HONESTLY? I WASN'T SURE IT WOULD WORK.

I SUPPOSE *THIS* IS A METAPHOR FOR US? FOR THE CORPS AND THE GUARDIANS LOSING SIGHT OF THE OTHER THREATS. I THINK YOU CAN DO BETTER, KYLE.

I WASN'T GOING TO LOOK A GIFT SPACE SHARK IN THE MOUTH. BUT I *AM* RIGHT.

KYLE, I SAID I WOULDN'T GIVE YOU ORDERS, AND I'M NOT. BUT I *NEED* YOU TO DO THIS.

BABY-SITTING? ANYONE CAN DO THAT.

NOT BABYSITTING. *GUARDING.* GUARDING *US* AGAINST *THEM.*

GANTHET WAS YOUR BEST FRIEND, AND THEY TURNED HIM INTO A TYRANT WHO TRIED TO KILL YOU.

YOU KNOW BETTER THAN ANYONE WHAT THE GUARDIANS ARE CAPABLE OF. WHAT HAPPENS WHEN THEY TURN ON US.

YOU'RE *RIGHT.* WE *HAVE* SPENT TOO MUCH TIME FIGHTING THEM. I NEED TIME TO REBUILD THIS CORPS.

AND THAT'S SOMETHING I *CAN'T* DO IF I HAVE TO BE LOOKING OVER MY SHOULDER.

SO YOU WANT *ME* TO WATCH THEM.

I DON'T TRUST THEM. I KNOW *YOU* WON'T TRUST THEM. AND I KNOW YOU'LL SEE IT COMING SOONER THAN ANYONE ELSE. AND, TRUTH BE TOLD, WITH YOUR POWER AS THE WHITE LANTERN...

YOU CAN *STOP* THEM. BUT I NEED YOU TO SAY YES.

...I'LL THINK ABOUT IT.

THIS IS THINKING ABOUT IT?

KYLE RAYNER'S APARTMENT. NEW YORK CITY.

NO, THIS IS *THOUGHT* ABOUT IT, CAROL. HAL WAS RIGHT.

I CAN'T BELIEVE YOU ACTUALLY JUST SAID THAT.

IT WAS A SURPRISE TO ME, TOO, BELIEVE ME.

I'M GOING TO ASSUME YOU'RE NOT TAKING ALL THIS JUNK WITH YOU?

WELL, YOU NEVER KNOW WHEN YOU'RE GOING TO NEED A LAVA LAMP IN DEEP SPACE...

NO. IT'S ALL GOING INTO STORAGE.

I PICKED THESE UP FOR THE FIRST TIME IN *MONTHS* LAST WEEK. I NEVER GET *BACK* HERE. I ALMOST FORGET WHAT IT'S LIKE, TO HAVE A LIFE OUTSIDE OF THE CORPS.

WHAT IS THIS "LIFE" OF WHICH YOU SPEAK? IT SOUNDS FAMILIAR...

SO. WHAT ARE YOU AND *HAL* GOING TO DO WHILE I PLAY TOUR GUIDE TO THE *BLUE MAN GROUP*?

HAL AND *I*? NOTHING.

SO YOU AND HAL...

THERE IS NO ME AND HAL. FOR THE MOMENT AT LEAST, THERE'S ME, AND THERE'S HAL.

I DIDN'T KNOW. HE DIDN'T SAY ANYTHING.

TO YOU? SHOCKING. HE BARELY SAID ANYTHING TO *ME* WHEN I TOLD HIM.

WHEN *YOU* TOLD *HIM*? I THOUGHT YOU LOVED HAL?

I DO, WHICH IS THE PROBLEM IN A NUTSHELL.

I *HAVE* TO LOVE HAL IF I WANT TO KEEP THIS. I CAN HELP A LOT OF PEOPLE WITH THIS STAR SAPPHIRE RING.

THE PROBLEM IS THAT I'VE COME TO REALIZE THAT I CAN'T LOVE HAL AND BE *WITH* HAL...

CAROL, I'M SORRY. REALLY, I...

SO...UH...DO YOU WANT TO TALK ABOUT IT?

NOPE.

PRETTY MUCH ANYTHING I SAY IS GOING TO MAKE THIS SUPER-AWKWARD, ISN'T IT?

YUP.

SO WHERE ARE THE BLUE CREW TAKING YOU?

THE EDGE OF THE UNIVERSE. LITERALLY.

THERE'S SOMETHING THERE THAT *WORRIED* THEM BEFORE THEY WERE LOCKED AWAY FOR MILLENNIA, AND THEY WANT TO INVESTIGATE IT.

SOMETHING THEY CALL...

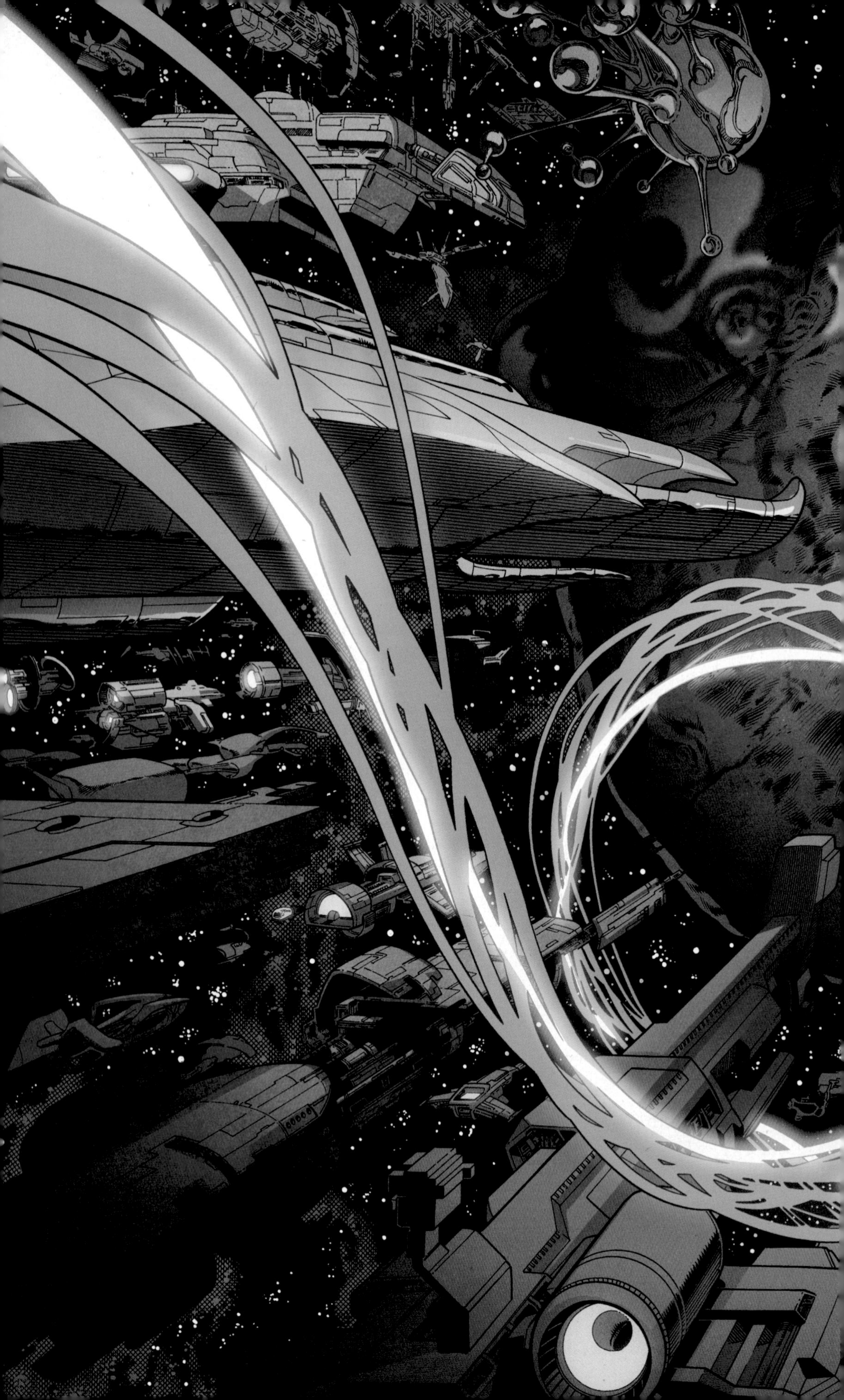

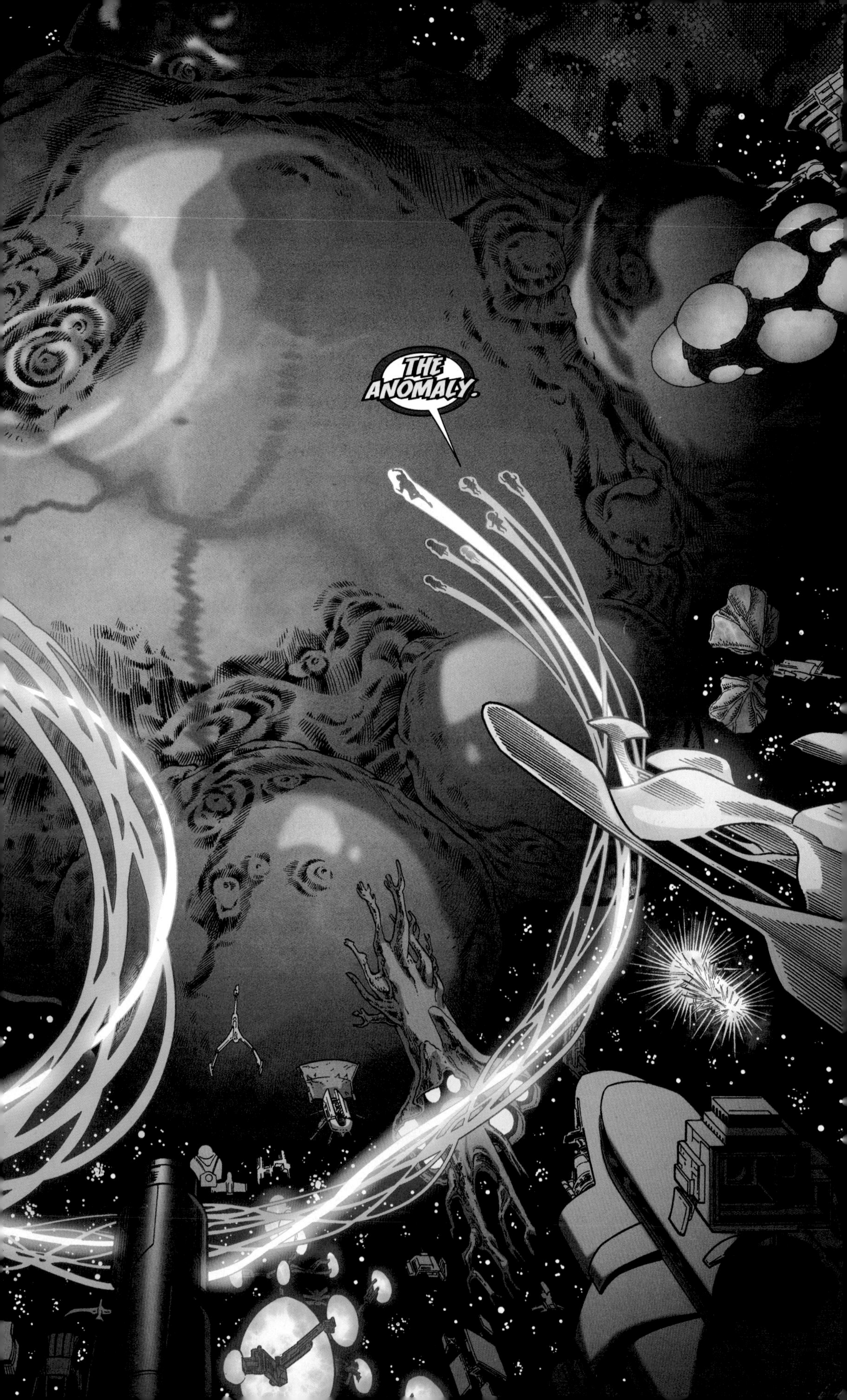
THE ANOMALY.

TERRIFIC. WHAT IS IT?

IF WE *KNEW* THAT, LANTERN RAYNER, WE WOULD NOT NEED TO COME HERE.

...MINE WOULD BE THAT THERE IS A FRAGMENT OF THE OLD UNIVERSE WITHIN.

"OLD" UNIVERSE...?

BEST GUESS?

WE ARE GUARDIANS. WE DO NOT "GUESS." WE KNOW OR WE DO NOT. AND WE WOULD *PREFER* TO KNOW.

BUT IF I WERE *NOT* A GUARDIAN, AND IF I *WERE* TO DO SOMETHING AS FOOLISH AS MAKING A GUESS...

I DO NOT BELIEVE OUR UNIVERSE WAS THE FIRST, NOR, QUITE LIKELY, WILL IT BE THE LAST. AND SOMETHING OF WHAT CAME BEFORE REMAINS HERE STILL.

THE ANOMALY.

NOT QUITE. WHAT YOU ARE SEEING AND SENSING IS, I THINK, OUR UNIVERSE *REACTION* TO THE OLD ONE...

...AN AREA OF SPACE-TIME SEALED AROUND THE DIFFERING PHYSICS.

A CYST.

PARDON?

IT'S A CYST IN THE FABRIC OF REALITY.

I SUPPOSE YOU MIGHT SAY THAT. AND I SUPPOSE YOU MIGHT SAY THAT WE ARE INTERESTED TO SEE IF IT IS *SAFE*, AND IF WE NEED INTERVENE.

IF YOU WERE TO GUESS.

WHICH I DO NOT DO.

OF COURSE NOT. AND ALL THESE SHIPS? WHAT DO *THEY* WANT?

THEY ARE SCANNING. *PROBING.* SO YES, I WOULD SAY THEIR PURPOSE IS THE SAME AS OURS.

BUT I DO NOT UNDERSTAND WHY THEY HAVE ONLY GONE SO CLOSE.

BROTHER...

SOMETHING IS HAPPENING.

THE SCIENTISTS ARE ALL *LEAVING.* HAS SOMETHING CHANGED WITHIN THE ANOMALY?

I HAVE DETECTED NO CHANGES.

NOR I.

HEH. YOU REALLY DON'T SEE IT, DO YOU?

I DO NOT UNDERSTAND, LANTERN RAYNER.

NO, YOU WOULDN'T, WOULD YOU? YES, PAALKO, SOMETHING HAS CHANGED.

YOU.

YOU DON'T THINK WHAT YOUR "BROTHERS" HAVE DONE IS NEWSWORTHY? YOU DON'T THINK THE UNIVERSE *KNOWS* WHAT THEY DID?

...THEY *FEAR* US.

YES.

AND THEY ARE RIGHT TO. BUT I DO NOT FEAR YOU, GUARDIAN.

I AM EXETER AND THIS IS THE BOUNDARY.

I GUESS WE KNOW WHY THE SHIPS DIDN'T GET CLOSER, THEN...

THIS PLACE IS DANGEROUS. AND THIS PLACE IS GLORIOUS. IT IS NOT FOR YOU, GUARDIANS. YOU MAY COME NO FURTHER.

ON WHOSE AUTHORITY?

AUTHORITY? WHAT AUTHORITY DID THESE CREATURES HAVE WHEN THEY DECIDE THE WHOLE OF EXISTENC WAS THEIRS TO POLICE?

THIS IS MY AUTHORITY AND YOU WILL GO NO FURTHER.

WE DO NOT WISH TO DISTURB IT. WE ONLY WISH TO *STUDY* IT. WE ARE NOT OUR BROTHERS. WE MEAN YOU, AND IT, NO HARM.

YOU MAY WISH AND YOU MAY MEAN, BUT YOU WILL GO NO FURTHER.

LANTERN RAYNER, PLEASE DEAL WITH THIS.

YEAH, YOU'RE NOT LIKE THE OLD GUARDIANS AT *ALL.*

NO.

WHOA THERE, GIGANTOR. THIS DOESN'T HAVE TO GO SOUR...

THEY CANNOT--

AND THEY WILL NOT.

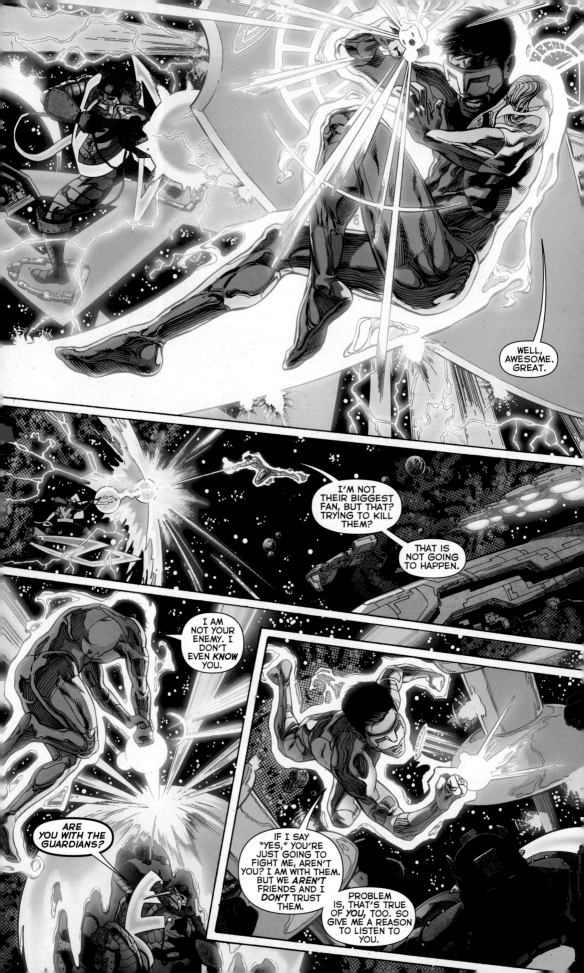

WELL, AWESOME. GREAT.

I'M NOT THEIR BIGGEST FAN, BUT THAT? TRYING TO KILL THEM?

THAT IS NOT GOING TO HAPPEN.

I AM NOT YOUR ENEMY. I DON'T EVEN *KNOW* YOU.

ARE YOU WITH THE GUARDIANS?

IF I SAY "YES," YOU'RE JUST GOING TO FIGHT ME, AREN'T YOU? I AM WITH THEM. BUT WE *AREN'T* FRIENDS AND I *DON'T* TRUST THEM.

PROBLEM IS, THAT'S TRUE OF *YOU*, TOO. SO GIVE ME A REASON TO LISTEN TO YOU.

THIS IS MY REASON. BECAUSE I CAN. AND BECAUSE I CAN, I MUST.

THAT'S PHILOSOPHICAL, BUT NOT HELPFUL. NOW...

...BACK OFF.

YOU DO NOT UNDERSTAND THE DANGER HERE.

WHAT IS WITHIN CANNOT BE UNDERSTOOD. WHAT CANNOT BE UNDERSTOOD WARPS.

AAAAH!

OKAY, SO YOU CAN THRO[W] MY POWER RIG[HT] BACK AT ME? GREAT.

THIS IS NOT RIGHT.

THE ANOMALY IS *CHANGING.*

IT IS NOT CHANGING, SISTER...

"IT IS *REACTING.*"

NO.

"NO" IS RIGHT. ARE YOU READY TO BE REASONABLE?

LANTERN RAYNER, RELEASE HIM! IT'S *YOU!*

WHAT DO YOU MEAN?

IT DOES NOT MATTER.

"THE POWER RING. THE ANOMALY IS REACTING TO IT. YOU MUST NOT USE IT!"

BEFORE IT IS TOO LATE-- THE INTEGRITY OF SPACE-TIME--

NO. IT IS ALREADY MUCH TOO LATE.

THIS, THEN, IS WHAT YOU REAP, YOU FOOLISH GUARDIANS...

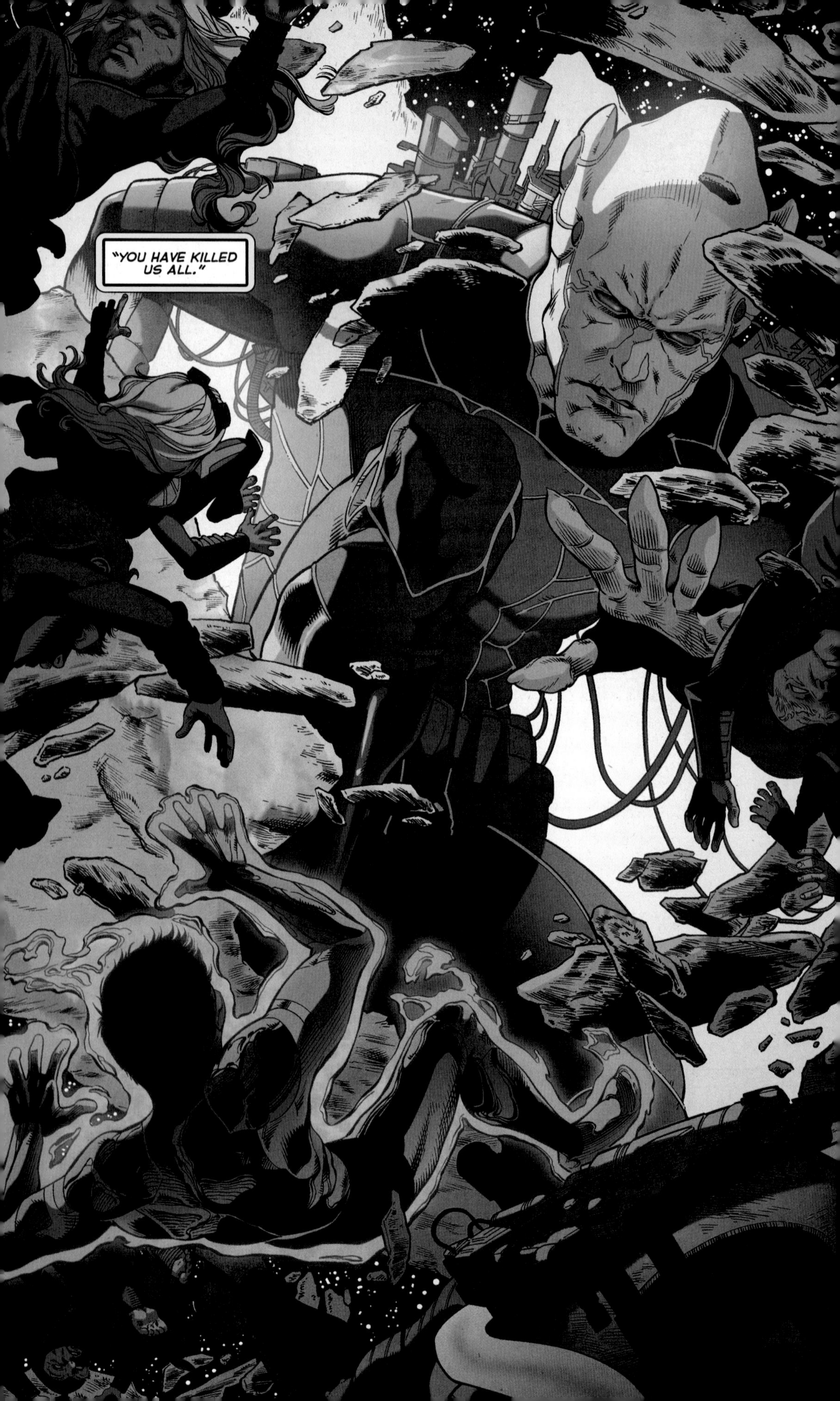
"YOU HAVE KILLED US ALL."

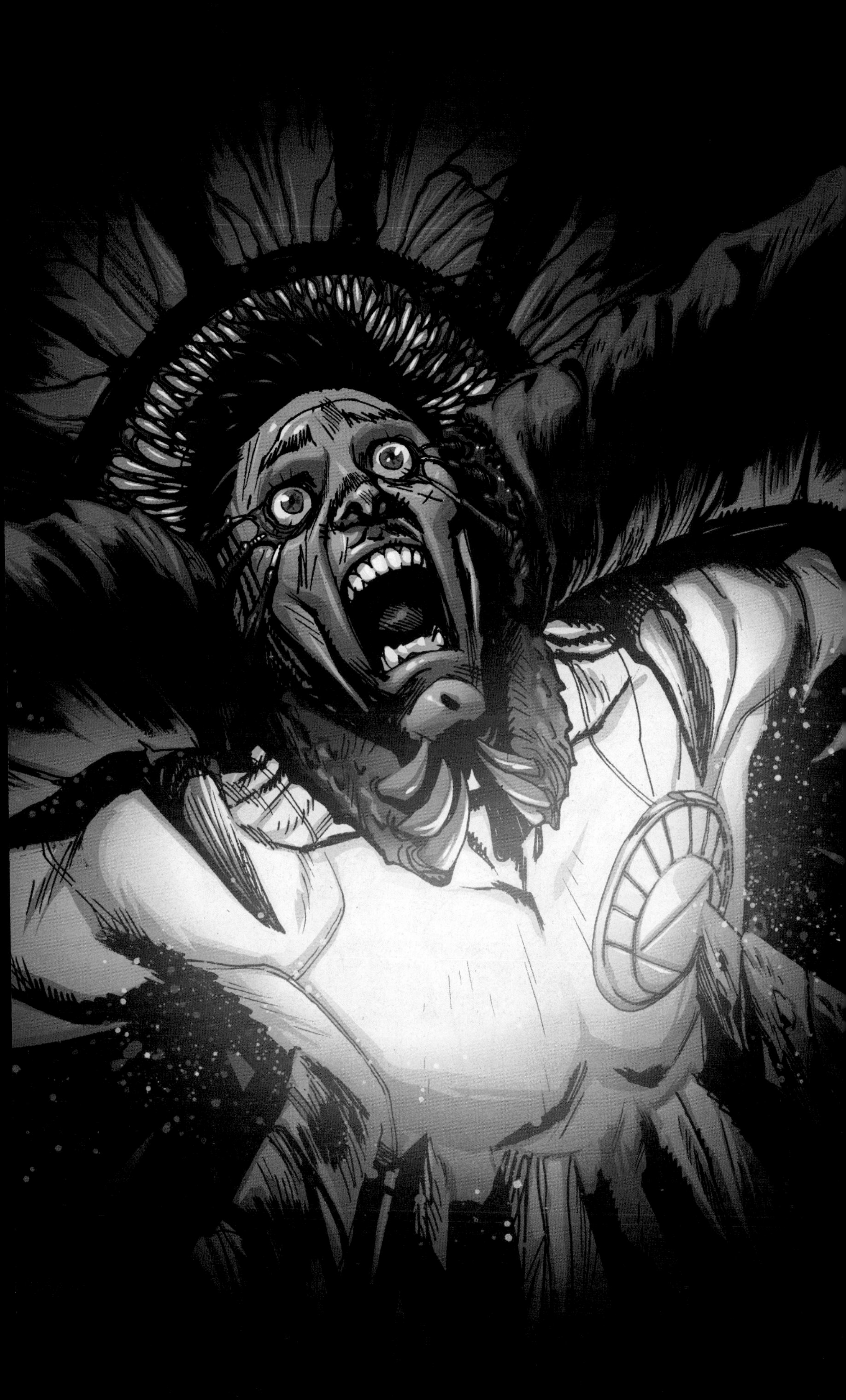

RELIC

JUSTIN JORDAN writer BRAD WALKER penciller ANDREW HENNESSY inker
cover art by RAFAEL ALBUQUERQUE & DAVE McCAIG RELIC variant cover by RAGS MORALES

LIVE AREA

CROP

I WONDER IF THE NEW GUARDIANS SYMPATHIZE...

<FASCINATING. I AM...ALIVE? >

THE EDGE OF THE UNIVERSE.

...WITH BEING RELEASED IN A UNIVERSE THAT YOU NO LONGER RECOGNIZE. A PLACE WHERE, PERHAPS, YOU DO NOT BELONG.

<THEN I WAS MISTAKEN.>

<THE COSMOS SURVIVED. THEY DID NOT DAMN US ALL...>

THE FIRST REACTION IS CONFUSION.

THEN CURIOSITY.

<NO, THE STARS ARE WRONG. THE PHYSICS ARE WRONG.>

<THIS IS... NEW. THIS IS WHAT CAME AFTER. ANOTHER UNIVERSE.>

<PROBES OUT. SEEK. LEARN.>

AND THEN?

YOU HAVE ANY IDEA WHAT THIS IS, PAALKO? WE CAN'T LET HIM HURT ALL THESE PEOPLE.

THIS IS NOT AN ATTACK, KYLE RAYNER. THIS IS... RESEARCH.

"THOSE DEVICES ARE SENDING OUT PINGS INTO THE QUANTUM STRUCTURE. THEY ARE RECORDING THE MAKEUP OF THE SHIPS AND THEIR CREW."

RELEASE ME.

DO YOU KNOW WHAT HE IS, EXETER??

HE IS THE LAST. A FOSSIL FROM THE OLD UNIVERSE.

YOU HAVE STUDIED HIM.

YES. AND KNOW THAT T UNIVERSE H CONTAINED INSIDE TH ANOMALY FO REASON.

SONOFA...

AND THIS CANNOT CONTINUE.

DO YOU HEAR ME?

EXETER, STOP. WE DON'T KNOW WHAT HE WANTS! DON'T--

MMRRRPPH

SSEES-THISS?

-PROVOKE HIM.

MONSTER, YOU WILL REMAIN HERE. YOU WILL CEASE THIS EXPLORATION AND YOU WILL--

<FEMTOTECHNOLOGY.>

<USEFUL.>

<SCAN AND REPLICATE-->

ZZZAK

<THE LIGHT? THEY ARE USING THE LIGHT!>

<SO THERE WILL BE A...>

<...LIGHTSMITH.>

I DON'T KNOW IF YOU CAN UNDERSTAND ME. THE RING SAYS IT HAS NO IDEA WHAT YOU'RE SAYING. BUT YOU NEED TO UNDERSTAND *THIS*--

LET HIM GO.

<NO, THIS WILL NOT HAPPEN AGAIN. THIS CANNOT HAPPEN AGAIN.>

<I WILL NOT ALLOW YOU TO BURN DOWN ANOTHER UNIVERSE IN YOUR ARROGANCE.>

<I CANNOT HOPE FOR ANOTHER SECOND CHANCE.>

YOU STILL WITH US, BIG MAN?

YES, BUT LOOK...

NOW WHAT?

THE RING TELLS ME THAT THE PROBES HAVE SUBVERTED THE SHIPS' INTERNAL NANO-REPAIR SYSTEMS. HE IS *CHANGING* THEM...

AND I DON'T NEED THE RING TO SEE THAT THE PEOPLE INSIDE ARE GOING TO *DIE* BEFORE HE'S FINISHED.

IT DOESN'T MATTER WHY HE'S DOING THIS, OR IF HE EVEN *KNOWS* HE'S KILLING THEM...

I HAVE TO STOP THIS.

YOU DO NOT KNOW WHAT HE IS CAPABLE OF--

I KNOW I'M NOT GOING TO LET THEM DIE. YOU AND THE OTHER LITTLE BOYS BLUE NEED TO GET THOSE PEOPLE OFF THOSE SHIPS. THIS IS NOT AN ARGUMENT.

WILL.

THEY'RE NOT WRONG. I DON'T KNOW WHAT I'M DEALING WITH.

BUT THEN, CERTAINTY WAS NEVER IN THE JOB DESCRIPTION.

AWESOME. I'VE BEEN EATEN BY A SPACESHIP.

PAALKO, CAN YOU HEAR ME? ANYONE?

I'M GOING TO TRY TO GET OUT OF...WHATEVER THIS IS.

COME ON, COME ON--

ARE THOSE THINGS... ABSORBING MY CONSTRUCT?

OH, THAT IS A BAD SIGN.

A VERY, VERY BAD SIGN.

WHEN I WAS LEARNING TO USE THE GREEN LANTERN RING, THE RESPONSIBILITY I HAD WAS SOMETHING THEY DRILLED INTO MY HEAD.

BECAUSE THEY WERE GIVING ME A *WEAPON. THE* WEAPON. THE MOST POWERFUL ONE IN THIS UNIVERSE.

BUT WHAT ABOUT THE *LAST* UNIVERSE?

HE'S DRAINING THE RING'S POWER AWAY AS FAST AS I CAN PROJECT IT.

I CAN'T...I CAN'T EVEN KEEP THE UNIFORM GOING...I--

NO!

NNAAAAHH

HOW CAN THERE POSSIBLY BE THIS MUCH FERRIS AIR PAPERWORK WHEN I *PAY* PEOPLE TO DO ALL THE PAPERWORK?

STAR SAPPHIRE, YOU ARE REQUIRED.

WHAT THE H--

NO.

YOU CAN'T

DO THIS.

WE WERE NOT SURE THAT WE COULD DO THIS *EITHER,* STAR SAPPHIRE. WERE IT NOT FOR YOUR *CONNECTION* TO LANTERN RAYNER, WE MIGHT NOT HAVE BEEN ABLE.

WHAT "CONNECTION"? WHAT ARE Y--

WE APOLOGIZE FOR THE ABRUPTNESS OF OUR MANNER, BUT WE DID NOT HAVE TIME TO WASTE.

HOW DID YOU DO THAT? HOW DID YOU HIJACK MY RING?

WE DID NOT HIJACK IT. WE ALTERED THE RING'S PROGRAMMING TO TEMPORARILY RESPOND TO OUR COMMAND. AND *NOT* WITHOUT DIFFICULTY.

KYLE WAS RIGHT, YOU'RE JUST LIKE THE OTHERS. YOU JUST PULL SOMEONE ACROSS THE UNIVERSE WITHOUT ASKING AND--

PLEASE...

...LOOK. SEE. AND PERHAPS *FORGIVE.* WE NEED ASSISTANCE, AND JUDGED YOU MOST ABLE.

WHAT IS *THIS?*

WE.....MADE AN ERROR. AND NOW LANTERN RAYNER IS PAYING FOR IT. AND WE NEED YOUR HELP.

WHERE *IS* KYLE?

DO YOU NEED ANYTHING, KYLE.

OKAY, SO I ALREADY DID THE ALPHABET... THE HISTORY OF THE CORPS... THE INTERGALACTIC ATLAS ... THE TOP TEN SCIENCE FICTION MOVIES OF THE SEVENTIES... AND, WELL, ALL THIS.

SO WHAT'S NEXT?

I'M PRETTY SURE I'M GOOD. I'M ALSO PRETTY SURE I'M DONE WITH THIS ONE.

PERHAPS YOU COULD PAINT ME A PICTURE OF... "OA."

YOU KNOW... I DON'T KNOW WHAT TO CALL YOU. YOU KNOW MY NAME, BUT...

...THEY CALLED ME RELIC.

BUT THEY ARE ALL DEAD NOW.

I'M SORRY.

I AM NOT.

OH, WELL... COOL. HUH...

DO YOU HEAR THAT?

WHAT, KYLE?

I COULD SWEAR I COULD HEAR SOMEONE SCREAMING.

CAN YOU?

INTERESTING.

NOW, SHOW ME MORE ABOUT THESE *BATTERIES...*

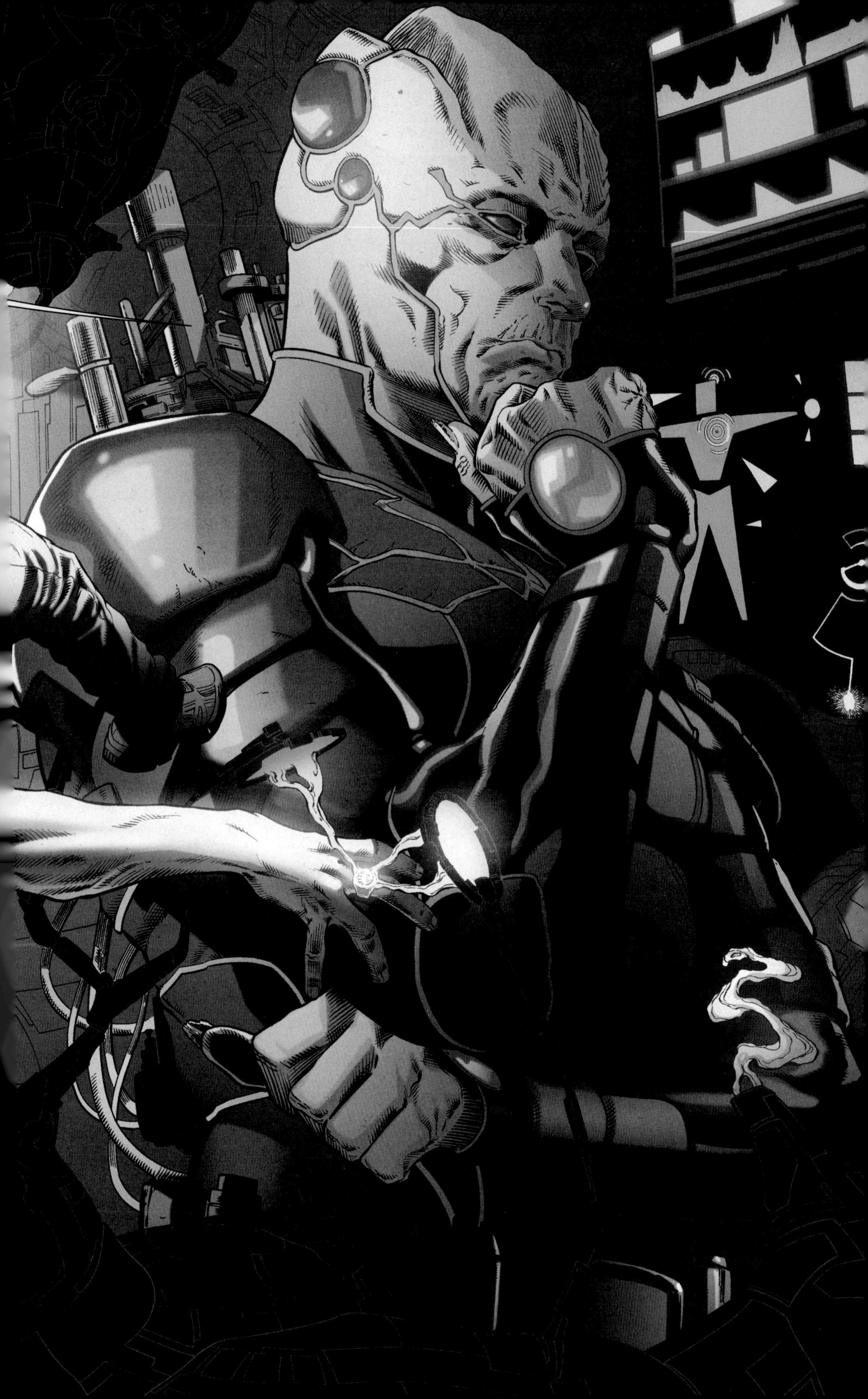

THEY STILL FEAR US. THEY *STRUGGLE.*

IF WE DO NOT MOVE THEM SOON, THEY WILL HURT THEMSELVES. BUT THERE ARE SO MANY OTHERS, AND WE CANNOT ABANDON LANTERN RAYNER...

THEN WE NEED TO STOP THIS AT THE SOURCE.

WE ARE *GOING* TO STOP THIS...AS SOON AS OUR NEW ALLY IS PREPARED.

I AM. WE MAY PROCEED, GUARDIAN. MY WEAPON IS REPAIRED. I CAN TAKE ANY ENERGY DIRECTED AGAINST ME AND RETURN IT IN KIND.

THIS MONSTER HAS STOLEN FROM ME. TURNED MY WEAPON AGAINST US. BUT LET US SEE...

HOW CLEVER HE IS.

I REALLY, REALLY HOPE THIS PLAN WORKS.

DO NOT WORRY...

...IT WILL.

I DO NOT KNOW IF YOUR RING CAN TRANSLATE THE TERM, BUT MY PEOPLE CALL THIS...

"FEEDBACK." NOW, CAROL FERRIS!

...HAVEN'T ACTUALLY BEEN HERE YET, BUT WALKER SAID THEY WERE CALLING IT "ELPIS"--

KYLE, CAN YOU HEAR ME?

CAROL?

COME TO WATCH THE MASTER AT WORK?

KYLE, I NEED YOU TO SNAP OUT OF THIS.

KYLE STILL HAS WORK TO DO.

HE'S RIGHT. I'M NOT FINISHED HERE.

KYLE, THIS ISN'T REAL.

OF COURSE IT IS...

NO. I....I DON'T UNDERSTAND.

FASCINATING.

KYLE, I NEED YOU TO WAKE UP. I NEED YOU TO...

WOULD I LIE TO YOU, KYLE? I CARE ABOUT YOU ENOUGH TO CONTACT YOU HERE. TO DO THIS. WOULD I DO THAT WITHOUT REASON? YOU KNOW ME, KYLE.

OPEN YOUR EYES.

THIS *ISN'T* REAL.

CAROL IS REAL.

I AM REAL.

AND I AM LEAVING.

I NEVER OBSERVED...

IMPOSSIBLE! THERE *IS* NO WHITE LIGHT!

HIT ME.

I DON'T WANT--

BETTER.

HIT ME.

I CAN FEEL CAROL, OUTSIDE, LIKE A BEACON, I GO FOR IT.

I HAVE REACHED MY LIMITS, CAROL FERRIS. HIS MACHINES ARE ADAPTING FASTER THAN I CAN DESTROY THEM.

FLEE.

HEY, CAROL.

HH-- HRRK... HELP--

NICE OF YOU TO JOIN US.

WE NEED TO GET SOME SPACE BETWEEN US AND THAT SHIP...

WE NEED *HELP.* WE NEED HAL, GUY, JOHN. WE NEED *EVERYONE.*

LANTERN RAYNER, LOOK...

HE IS RETREATING. WE HAVE WON.

NO. WE HAVEN'T.

HE WANTED TO KNOW ABOUT THE *RINGS,* ALL OF THEM, EVERY COLOR OF THE SPECTRUM. HE *HATES* THEM. AND NOW HE KNOWS EVERYTHING I KNOW ABOUT THEM.

HIS NAME IS *RELIC.* AND HE'S NOT RETREATING. HE'S FINISHED HERE. HE LEARNED ALL HE COULD FROM US. WE'RE JUST A *DISTRACTION.*

HE WANTS TO *DESTROY* THE RINGS. AND I'VE NEVER SEEN ANYTHING LIKE HIM. THE INTELLIGENCE. THE WILL.

I.... I DON'T KNOW IF WE CAN STOP HIM.

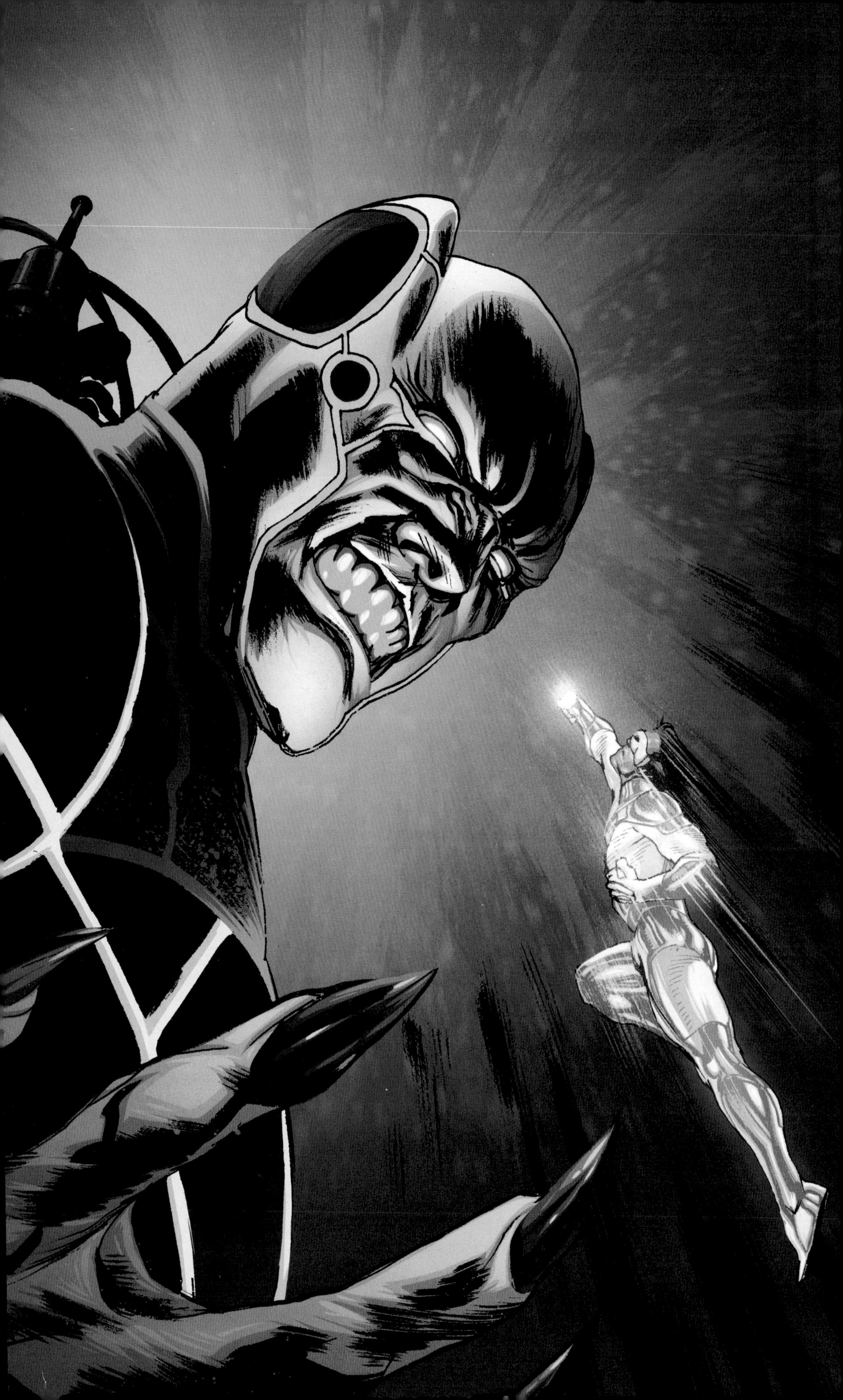

KEEP HOPE ALIVE

JUSTIN JORDAN writer **BRAD WALKER** penciller **ANDREW HENNESSY** inker
cover art by **RAFAEL ALBUQUERQUE & DAVE McCAIG** RELIC variant cover by **RAGS MORALES**

NEW HOME OF THE BLUE LANTERNS.

...THE WHITE LANTERN, I CAN CHANNEL ALL THE ENERGIES OF THE EMOTIONAL SPECTRUM, AND HAVE ACCESS TO THE UNIQUE ABILITIES THAT COME WITH EACH OF THEM.

BUT IT MIGHT SURPRISE YOU WHICH ONE I CONSIDER THE GREATEST-- THE BLUE LIGHT OF HOPE.

EVEN AFTER THEIR HOME PLANET WAS TAKEN FROM THEM BY THE REACH, THE BLUE LANTERNS FOUND A NEW PLANET AND MADE IT THEIR HOME.

THEY NEVER STOPPED BELIEVING, EVEN FOR A SECOND, THAT "ALL WOULD BE WELL."

I'VE ALWAYS ADMIRED THEIR FAITH, AND I WISH THAT THERE MORE THAN JUST THIS HANDFUL OF THEM...

...THE UNIVERSE COULD USE MORE BEINGS LIKE THE BLUE LANTERNS.

OH!

IS SOMETHING WRONG, SAINT WALKER?

YES, WARTH...

ADARA!

...SOMETHING IS VERY WRONG.

IF THE ENTITY IS A LIVING *REPRESENTATION* OF OUR CORPS...

...WHAT DOES IT MEAN IF SHE GETS *SICK?*

I TRULY DO NOT KNOW.

SHOULD WE FOLLOW HER, TRY TO HELP HER?

I AM NOT CERTAIN THAT WE COULD. I AM, HOWEVER, CERTAIN...

WE HAVE OTHER PROBLEMS.

SO IT DOESN'T *SURPRISE ME...*

...THAT *RELIC* CAME *HERE* FIRST.

THE BLUE LANTERNS' RINGS CAN *SUPER-CHARGE* THE GREEN LANTERN RINGS. CONSIDERING THAT POWER, AND THEIR SMALL NUMBERS...

...THIS IS WHERE I WOULD START IF I WANTED TO TEAR DOWN THE CORPS.

REMAIN CALM, BROTHERS AND SISTERS.

WE ARE NOT YOUR ENEMY. WHATEVER IT IS THAT YOU ARE DOING--

YES. THAT WOULD BE HELPFUL IN THIS PROCESS.

DO YOU *KNOW* WHAT I'M DOING? OR DO YOU *HOPE?*

I DO NOT KNOW WHO YOU ARE. BUT I AM NOT AN IDIOT.

I AM ASKING YOU TO STOP. AND THAT IS THE LAST TIME I WILL *ASK.*

I *KNOW* YOUR KIND, LIGHTSMITH. YOU HAVE NO OFFENSIVE ABILITIES WITHOUT THE LIGHT OF *RESOLVE.*

I HAD HOPED NOT TO FIGHT YOU...

WALKER... HE IS *DRAINING* THE BATTERY!

INTERESTING. YET YOU DON'T *ATTACK.*

AND WE WILL NOT. PLEASE, WE DO NOT HAVE TO BE ENEMIES. WE ARE...

I KNOW WHAT YOU ARE. AND YOU *ARE* THE ENEMY-- OF EVERYTHING THAT LIVES.

BUT THAT DOESN'T MEAN I CANNOT.

WILLPOWER DETECTED.

I'D HAVE LIKED TO HAVE GOTTEN HERE SOONER...

...BUT BETTER LATE THAN NEVER.

THAT WAS FORTUITOUS TIMING, KYLE.

I TRIED TO SEND A MESSAGE THROUGH THE RINGS, BUT HE'S BLOCKING THEM SOMEHOW.

HE IS *INTERFERING* WITH THE ENERGY OF THE RINGS. NOTHING GETS PAST HIM. WE HAD TO TRACE HIS TUNNEL THROUGH SPACETIME JUST TO FOLLOW HIM HERE.

HMMM.

I WISH I HAD MORE TIME FOR PLEASANTRIES, CAROL FERRIS--BUT I CAN FEEL OUR LIGHT FADING FROM THE BATTERY.

STOP, RELIC. THEY HAVEN'T HURT YOU. THEY HAVEN'T HURT *ANYONE.*

I KNOW. WE NEED TO FIND A WAY TO *SEVER* THAT CONNECTION.

I WISH THAT WERE TRUE.

"BUT EVERY SECOND, THEY PROVE HOW DANGEROUS THEY ARE, DRIVING THIS UNIVERSE THAT MUCH CLOSER TO THE END."

FOCUS ALL YOUR ENERGY ON THE DEVICES!

THEY CAN ABSORB WHAT WE PUT OUT, BUT WE MIGHT BE ABLE TO *OVERLOAD* HIS SYSTEM...

THIS IS NOT WORKING.

PERHAPS WHAT WE NEED IS A *DIRECT* APPROACH.

WARTH, WHAT ARE YOU...

UNNNFFFFF!

WHAT?

AH. WELL, YES.

THAT IS CERTAINLY ONE WAY TO CUT THE GORDIAN KNOT.

I DON'T BELIEVE YOU'RE SO FOOLISH AS TO THINK YOU CAN HARM ME WITH YOUR RINGS, LIGHTSMITHS.

US, NO...

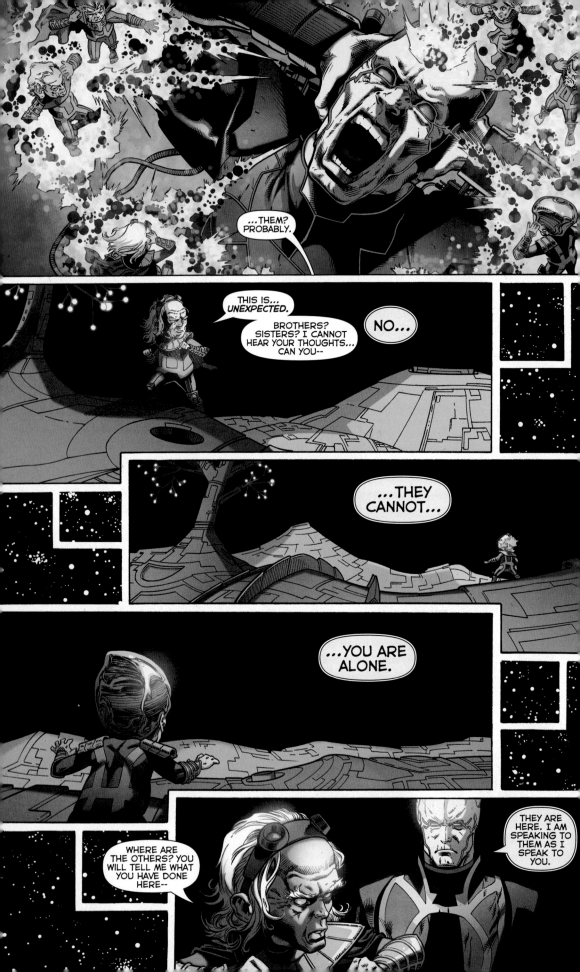

...THEM? PROBABLY.

THIS IS... UNEXPECTED.

BROTHERS? SISTERS? I CANNOT HEAR YOUR THOUGHTS... CAN YOU--

NO...

...THEY CANNOT...

...YOU ARE ALONE.

WHERE ARE THE OTHERS? YOU WILL TELL ME WHAT YOU HAVE DONE HERE--

THEY ARE HERE. I AM SPEAKING TO THEM AS I SPEAK TO YOU.

THAT IS IMPOSSIBLE.

CLEARLY NOT. YOU THINK SO SLOWLY. IN THE SPACES BETWEEN YOUR THOUGHTS THERE'S AMPLE TIME FOR ME TO SPEAK TO THE OTHERS.

PERHAPS I WAS RASH. PERHAPS YOU CAN BE MADE TO UNDERSTAND. PERHAPS YOU CAN SEE.

SEE.

FEEL.

UNDERSTAND.

NO.

THAT-- THAT CANNOT BE.

NO--

NOOO!

KYLE, WHAT EXACTLY WAS THAT?

I REALLY WISH I KNEW, BRO'DEE. I WAS EXPECTING THEM TO ATTACK HIM, BUT THAT WAS.... I THINK THEY WERE TRYING TO READ HIS MIND.

CAN THEY DO THAT?

I HONESTLY DON'T KNOW. BUT IT'S DEFINITELY TIME FOR PLAN... UH...E? CAROL?

I GOT THIS.

PASSION?

NO.

CAROL, WHAT IS IT? CAN HE EVEN *FEEL* LOVE?

IT'S NOT THAT. IT *IS* LOVE, HE'S DOING THIS *BECAUSE* OF LOVE.

FOR WHAT?

EVERYTHING.

IF LOVE DOESN'T WORK...

THEN MAYBE *FEAR* WILL!

I DON'T *KNOW* WHAT RELIC FEARS. OR I DIDN'T.

BUT THE *RING* DOES.

AM I SUPPOSED TO *RETREAT* FROM TERROR?

ME, WHO HAS *SEEN* HIS WORST FEAR *REALIZED?*

NO.

WALKER, THERE ARE TOO MANY. THESE LITTLE MOSQUITOS ARE SUCKING THE BATTERY DRY.

THAT SHOULDN'T BE POSSIBLE. THE WHOLE *POINT* OF A CENTRAL BATTERY IS TO STAY CHARGED!

JUST *FOCUS* YOUR ENERGY--MAYBE WE CAN DESTROY THEM BY HITTING THEM WITH MORE THAN ONE SPECTRUM--!

I WISH YOU WOULD UNDERSTAND WHAT A *WASTE* THIS IS. WHAT A PRECIOUS RESOURCE YOU CHOOSE TO *SQUANDER.*

CAROL, WATCH OUT, HE'S RE-DIRECTING--

I'M OKAY, BUT--

WALKER!

AND THEN I REALIZE THE GAME.

HE WILL TURN *EVERYTHING* AGAINST US. EVEN HOPE.

NO!

YES.

AND YOU WILL LOSE EVEN THAT.

I CANNOT ALLOW ANOTHER UNIVERSE TO END BECAUSE OF YOUR ARROGANCE.

THE BATTERY IS *EMPTY*, BROTHERS. THE RINGS ARE ALL WE HAVE!

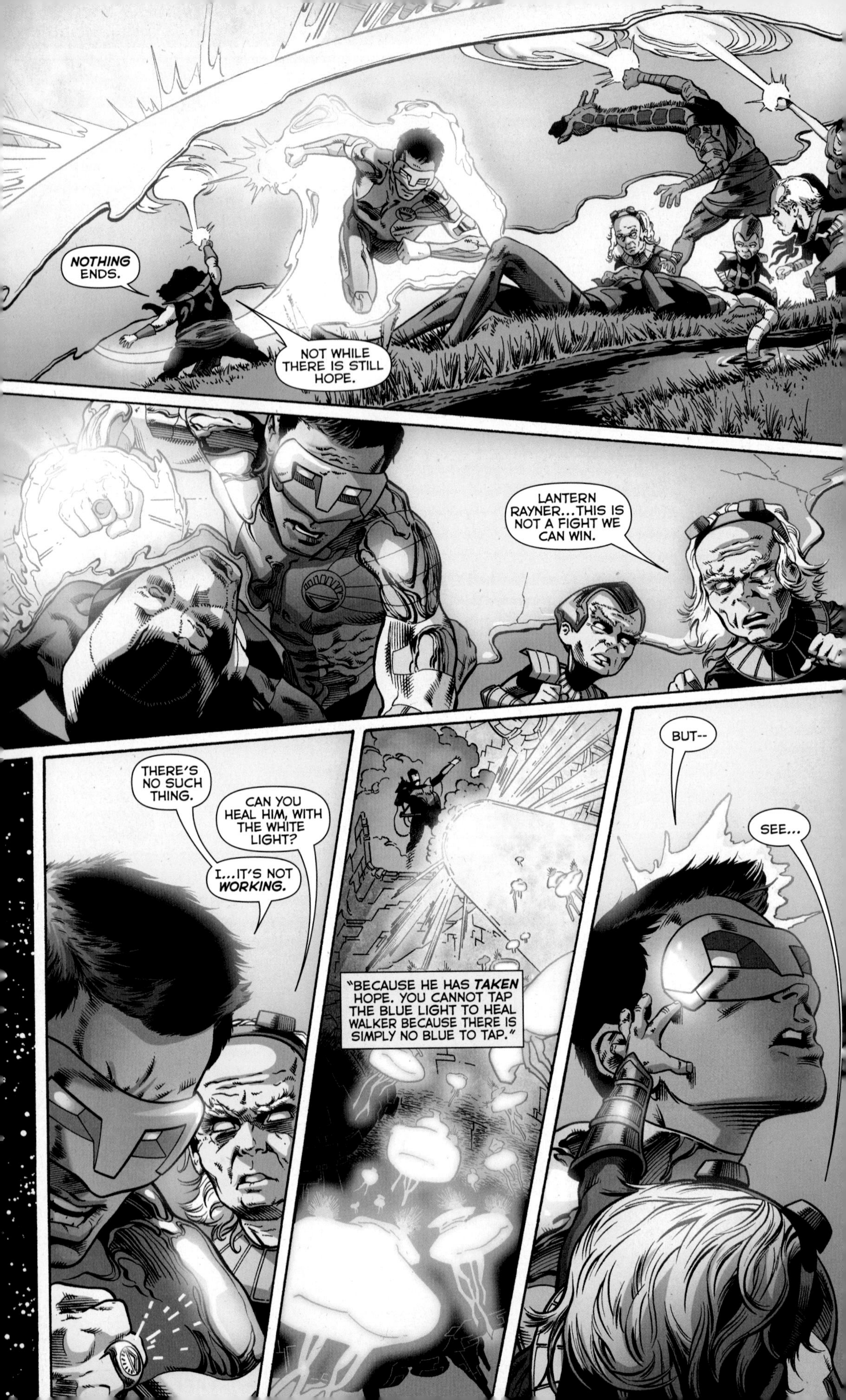
NOTHING ENDS.
NOT WHILE THERE IS STILL HOPE.
LANTERN RAYNER...THIS IS NOT A FIGHT WE CAN WIN.
THERE'S NO SUCH THING.
CAN YOU HEAL HIM, WITH THE WHITE LIGHT?
I...IT'S NOT WORKING.
"BECAUSE HE HAS TAKEN HOPE. YOU CANNOT TAP THE BLUE LIGHT TO HEAL WALKER BECAUSE THERE IS SIMPLY NO BLUE TO TAP."
BUT--
SEE...

...AND ...NDERSTAND.

...AND I DO. EVERYTHING RELIC IS, ...VERYTHING THE GUARDIANS SAW ...N HIS HEAD, IS LAID OUT BEFORE ...ME. AND I DO UNDERSTAND.

...HERE IS ...O HOPE.

NO. WE NEED TO...WE HAVE TO GET TO OA.

WE ARE RUNNING OUT OF TIME, BROTHER...

THEN GET ...S THERE, KYLE. ...U CAN USE THE ...DIGO ENERGY ...O TELEPORT US THERE.

I CAN'T. RELIC'S DRAINED SO MUCH POWER, AND I'VE NEVER TRANSPORTED SO MANY PEOPLE...I CAN'T MAKE THIS LEAP.

YES, BROTHER. YOU CAN... YOU WILL.

I WON'T LEAVE YOU.

YOU SAID IT YOURSELF, YOU CANNOT TAKE US WITH YOU. AND I WILL NOT CEDE *ANOTHER* HOME TO MONSTERS. TAKE SAINT WALKER.

THERE ARE SECRETS EVEN THE WHITE LANTERN DOES NOT KNOW...THIS IS ONE.

WILL.

POWER LEVEL 154%

COMPASSION.

POWER LEVEL 180%

THE BLUE LIGHT CAN CHARGE *MORE* THAN JUST WILL? HOW ARE YOU *DOING* THIS?

JUST *KEEP HOPE ALIVE*, KYLE RAYNER.

POWER LEVEL 0%

IT IS DONE.

AS ARE YOU. DO YOU BELIEVE YOUR SACRIFICE WILL CHANGE ANYTHING?

I HOPE SO. DO WHAT YOU CAME HERE TO DO.

ALL WILL BE WELL.

YES...

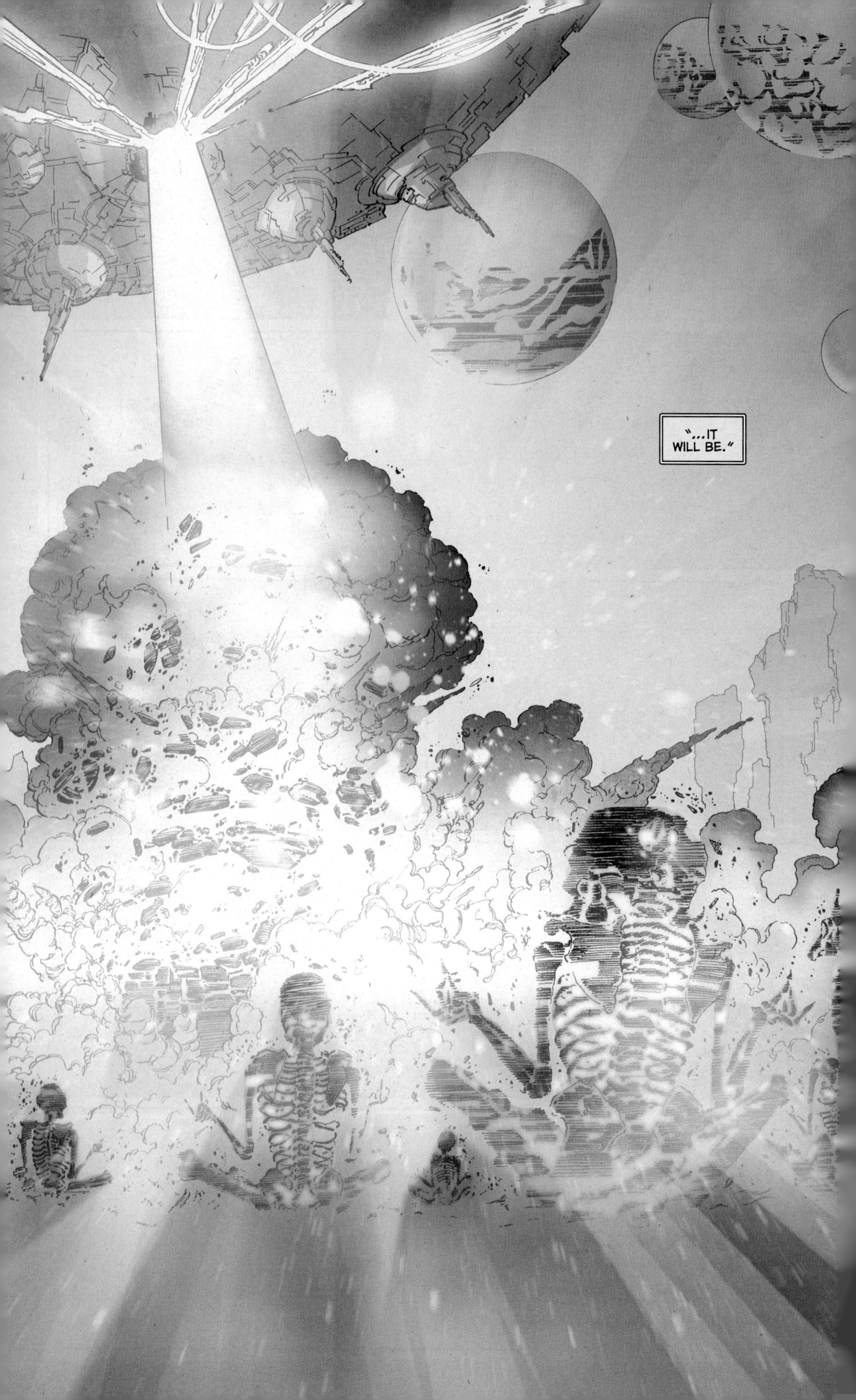
"...IT WILL BE."

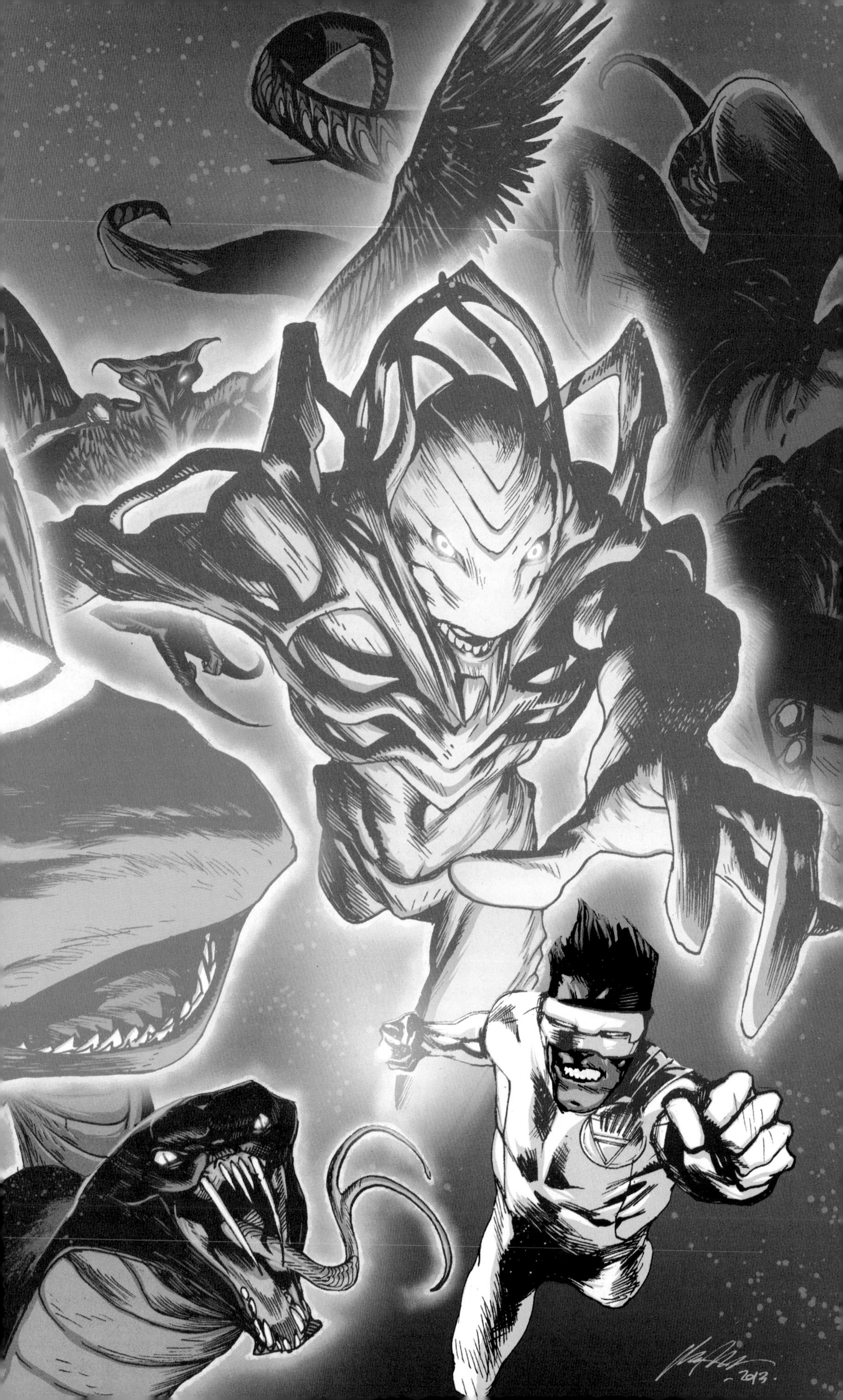

GODS AND MONSTERS
JUSTIN JORDAN writer BRAD WALKER penciller ANDREW HENNESSY, MARC DEERING & RYAN WINN inkers
cover art by RAFAEL ALBUQUERQUE & DAVE McCAIG

SECTOR ZERO.

THIS WAS OA.

FOR BILLIONS OF YEARS, IT WAS THE HOME PLANET OF THE GUARDIANS. THE HOME OF THE GREEN LANTERN CORPS. AT ITS BEST, IT WAS A BEACON OF HOPE FOR THE UNIVERSE.

OA WAS MEANT TO STAND FOR ALL ETERNITY.

ETERNITY ENDED TODAY.

NO.

THIS IS NOT... THIS IS NOT *POSSIBLE.*

NO.

HAL...

NO! NOT LIKE THIS. NOT UNDER *MY* WATCH.

CORPS, REGROUP AND PREPARE YOURSELF. WE ARE GOING TO *GET* THIS MONSTER--

NO.

WHAT DID YOU SAY?

I SAID *NO*, LANTERN JORDAN.

UNDERSTAND THIS, PAALKO. YOU DIDN'T *WANT* THIS JOB, SO YOU GAVE IT TO *ME*.

AND IF I AM IN CHARGE OF THE CORPS--OR WHAT'S LEFT OF IT--I WON'T HAVE YOU COUNTERMANDING MY ORDERS. OR YOU CAN FIND SOMEONE ELSE FOR THE JOB.

I JUST LOST THE HOME I HAVE DREAMED OF FOR *BILLIONS* OF YEARS. I HAVE ALREADY LOST MY BROTHERS AND SISTERS.

I WILL NOT LOSE THE CORPS.

WE CAN'T--

WE AREN'T. HAL, WE *AREN'T* LETTING HIM GO. BUT WE CAN'T FIGHT EACH OTHER *AND* RELIC.

WE LOST JOHN. WE LOST OA. WE LOST *EVERYTHING*.

BUT WE HAVEN'T *LOST*. NOT YET. IF YOU DO THIS, IF YOU JUST GO AFTER HIM, WE WILL.

HE KNOWS HOW THE RINGS WORK, HE KNOWS HOW THE BATTERIES WORK, AND HE KNOWS HOW TO DESTROY US. WE'VE ALREADY TRIED ALMOST EVERY SPECTRUM AGAINST HIM, AND WE'VE BARELY SLOWED HIM DOWN.

WE NEED A BETTER PLAN.

KYLE'S RIGHT.

THOSE LANTERNS ARE DEPENDING ON YOU, HAL. YOU SAY YOU'RE IN CHARGE OF THE CORPS?

THEN LEAD. BUT *DON'T* LEAD THEM INTO A FIGHT THEY CAN'T WIN.

...OKAY.

ALL RIGHT. THEN WHAT DO WE DO? HE'S GOT TO BE COMING FOR US...

I DO NOT BELIEVE THAT HE IS. IF HE WERE, HE WOULD HAVE COME IMMEDIATELY. WE'VE BECOME A *SECONDARY* CONCERN.

WE'RE RUNNING OUT OF POWER. ALL WE HAVE IS THE CHARGE THE RINGS STILL HAVE, AND I CAN TELL WE'RE RUNNING ON EMPTY.

THE CORPS IS. BUT THAT DOESN'T MEAN EVERYONE IS.

GEAR UP, LANTERNS. WE'RE HEADING TO YSMAULT.

WE'RE GOING TO GO TALK TO THE *RED* LANTERNS.

...I DO NOT KNOW IF THAT IS AN ADVISABLE COURSE OF ACTION.

I THINK THAT HE'S OUT OF HIS DAMN *MIND.*

I'M NOT. I SENT *GUY* UNDERCOVER WITH THE REDS. THEY'LL LISTEN TO HIM. HE'LL LISTEN TO ME.

...THE RED LANTERNS DO NOT DERIVE *ALL* THEIR ENERGY FROM A BATTERY. THEIR RINGS AND THEIR POWER ARE A MIXTURE OF TECHNOLOGY AND MAGIC.

RELIC IS SCIENTIFIC, METHODICAL, LOGICAL. HE MAY NOT BE PREPARED FOR SUCH A MIX.

AND THEY ARE ALWAYS, *ALWAYS* LOOKING FOR A FIGHT. I SAY WE SHOW THEM THE BIGGEST FIGHT IMAGINABLE.

I--

KYLE?!

THEY'RE COMING.

ION.
WILLPOWER.

ADARA.
HOPE.

PREDATOR.
LOVE.

THE ENTITIES.

OPHIDIAN. GREED.

THE ENTITY. LIFE.

PROSELYTE. COMPASSION.

THIS WILL DO.

I DON'T SUPPOSE YOU'D LIKE TO TRY TO EXPLAIN THIS?

I...

TERRIFIC. THAT'S THE HELPFUL GUARDIANS I'VE COME TO KNOW AND LOVE.

HAL...

HE... THEY...KYLE IS LEAVING.

THE HELL "THEY" ARE.

YOU NEED TO STOP--AND THEN YOU NEED TO TELL US WHAT IS GOING ON.

WHY ARE YOU ALL HERE? WHAT IS GOING ON WITH THE RINGS? WHAT DID YOU DO TO RAYNER?

FINE. HAVE IT YOUR WAY.

HOLD ON. LET ME TRY SOMETHING BEFORE YOUR TESTOSTERONE GETS US STEAMROLLED...

THIS WORKED LAST TIME.

KYLE, IF YOU CAN--

WE CAN ALL HEAR YOU. AND WHILE I LOVE YOU, STAR SAPPHIRE...

...YOUR PRESENCE IS NO LONGER REQUIRED. NONE OF YOU ARE. OUR PURPOSE IS CLEAR.

I CAN'T... CAN'T MOVE. I CAN'T USE THE RING--

YOU ARE NOT LEAVING.

CORPS...

"KICK THEIR COLLECTIVE ASS."

HAL JORDAN. YOU CANNOT THINK TO HOLD US AGAINST OUR WILL?

I THINK YOU NEED TO EXPLAIN YOURSELVES.

I THINK RELIC IS KILLING YOU ALL, SOMEHOW. SO WHY DON'T YOU TALK TO US? HELP US? BECAUSE WE DAMN WELL NEED SOME.

CAN'T...

HE'S TOO STRONG. WE'RE...

YOU ARE RUNNING OUT OF POWER. I DO NOT THINK THIS WOULD BE FRUITFUL EVEN IF YOU HAD THE FULL CAPABILITIES OF THE RINGS, AND THE FULL MIGHT OF THE CORPS. BUT YOU DO NOT.

YOUR WILL IS THE REASON YOU WEAR THAT RING, JORDAN. DO NOT LET IT BE THE REASON THE CORPS DIES.

NO. *NO.* THEY CAN HELP US BEAT RELIC, THEY CAN--

ENOUGH.

RELIC IS NOT OUR CONCERN. IT IS NOT HE WHO HAS WEAKENED US, LANTERN.

NOT YOUR CONCERN? *NOT YOUR CONCERN?!* HE *ANNIHILATED* OA. HE *MURDERED* THE BLUE LANTERNS. AND YOU AREN'T *CONCERNED?*

WE CAN STILL WIN THIS. BUT WE NEED TO WORK TOGETHER. WE NEED TO GO TO YSMAULT...

THIS IS BIGGER THAN YOU, LANTERN. YOU CANNOT AID US OR DELAY US.

AND AS FOR YSMAULT, IF THAT IS WHERE YOU WISH TO SPEND WHAT MAY BE YOUR FINAL MOMENTS...

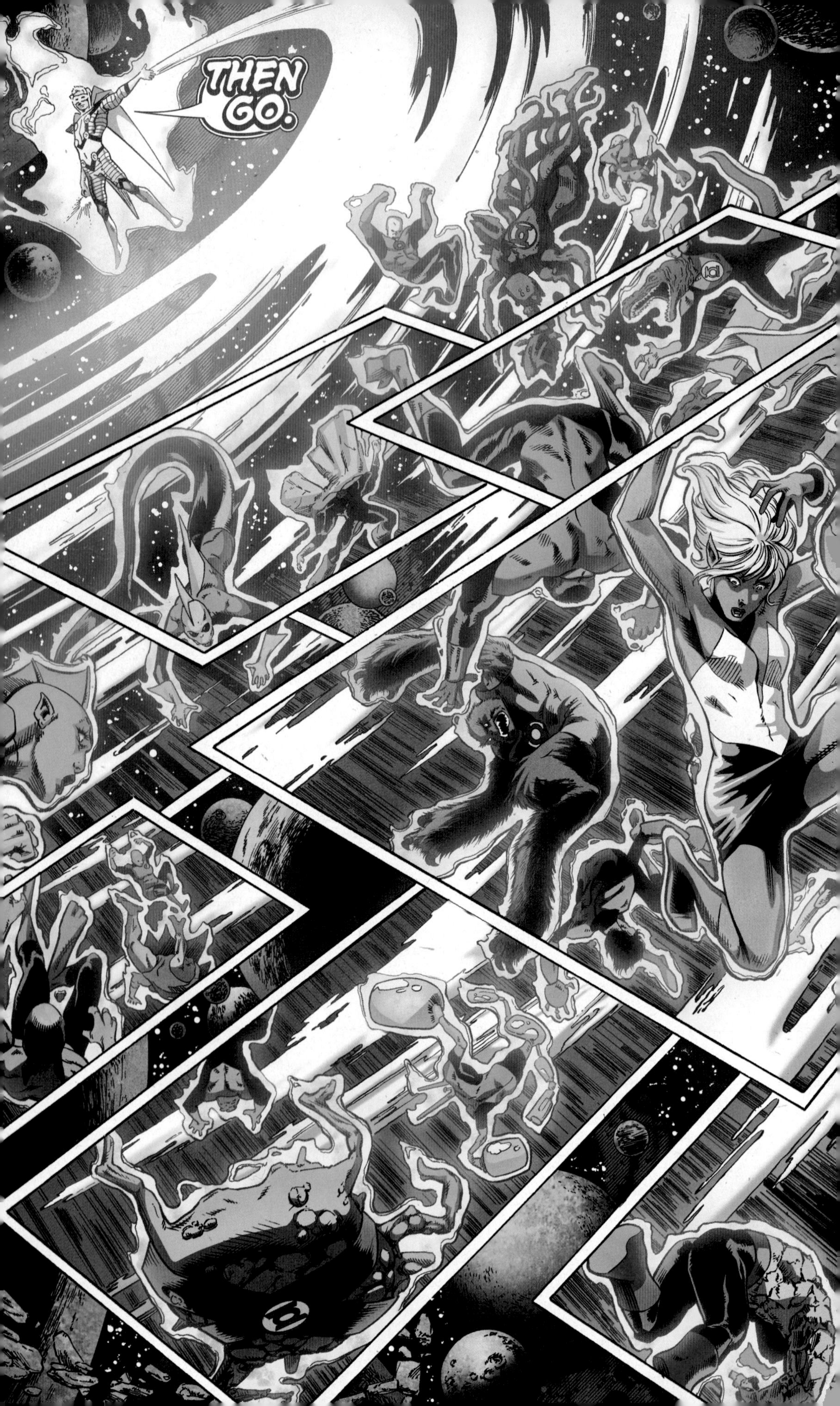
THEN GO.

OKAY, WHAT JUST HAPPENED?

I'M PRETTY SURE WE CAUGHT THE FAST TRAIN TO YSMAULT.

AND WE'RE SO LOW ON POWER, THERE'S NO GOING *BACK*...

KYLE'S ON HIS OWN.

THE PLANET ISN'T HERE, LANTERN STEWART. HE MUST HAVE DESTROYED IT ALREADY! WE CAN'T... WE CAN'T BEAT HIM...

ROOKIE, YOU NEED TO MUSTER UP THE *WILL* TO PULL YOURSELF TOGETHER BEFORE YOU...

--HRRRK--

...LOSE CONTROL OF THE RING.

I REALIZE YOU'RE NEW AT THIS. BUT I'M NOT. HAVE SOME FAITH. THE PLANET IS HERE. YOU JUST NEED TO KNOW THE MAGIC WORDS.

NOK NOK

HUH. I REALLY DON'T BELIEVE THAT WORKED.

WHAT WORKED?

WELL, ON MY PLANET, "KNOCK KNOCK" IS...YOU KNOW WHAT, IT DOESN'T MATTER.

IT'S ALL IN HOW YOU SAY IT.

THERE'S A WHOLE PLANET FOR THEM TO HIDE ON. SO HOW DO WE FIND THEM?

I WOULDN'T WORRY ABOUT IT.

THEY'LL FIND US.

NOK?

PLEASE, TAKE US TO INDIGO-1...

...UNLESS ONE OF YOU IS NATROMO?

WE ARE INCOMPLETE.

WE ARE.

THEY CANNOT RESIST THE CALL.

NOT ALONE.

BUT THEY ARE *NOT* ALONE. *PARALLAX* IS TRAPPED--THE SERVANT OF THE SINGLE MOST INDOMITABLE WILL IN CREATION. AND WHERE THAT WILL HAS TAKEN HIM....EVEN WE CANNOT SENSE. HE IS LOST TO US.

BUT THE *BUTCHER...*

THE BUTCHER WISHES TO COME. HE IS NEAR. AND HE IS ANGRY.

HE IS ALWAYS ANGRY. THAT IS HIS PURPOSE.

WE MUST *ALL* BE HERE. WE MUST FIND THEM.

THE BUTCHER, I BELIEVE WE CAN AID. AND WE WILL.

ALL.

...SOMETHING IS WRONG.

ALL WILL BE WELL.

IT IS THE *VESSEL*.

I CAN'T BEGIN TO DESCRIBE THIS. THEY'RE...*VAST*. IMAGINE TRYING TO FIGHT THE OCEAN. THEN IMAGINE TRYING TO FIGHT *SIX* OF THEM.

HE VESSEL'S WILL S ADMIRABLE BUT MISGUIDED.

THIS SHOULD NOT BE POSSIBLE. HE IS...

HUMAN. IT IS NOT COINCIDENCE THAT SO MANY OF THEM WIELD OUR RINGS SO WELL...

THEY FLOOD AGAINST ME. WHEN I HAVE ONE CONTAINED, THE OTHERS OVERWHELM ME. I CAN'T...

NOR *SHOULD* YOU. WE *WILL* DO THIS.

WE *LOVE* YOU, KYLE.

WE *FEEL* FOR YOU.

WE *WANT* YOU.

BUT WE HOPE YOU UNDERSTAND. YOU ARE JUST ONE PERSON. YOU ARE...

...ALONE.

NO...

...YOU CERTAINLY ARE NOT.

YOU DO NOT UNDERSTAND. YOU CANNOT HOPE TO STOP US.

CAN'T WE?

THEN HOW ARE WE HERE? HOW DID WE RESIST YOUR POWER BEFORE, THAT TOOK THE REST TO YSMAULT?

IT IS *YOU* WHO DO NOT UNDERSTAND. YOU HAVE OUR FRIEND. AGAINST HIS WILL, AGAINST HIS WISHES. THIS IS *UNACCEPTABLE.*

WE WERE OLD WHEN THE UNIVERS WAS YOUNG. WE HA SEEN THE VERY HAN OF CREATION.

AND YOU WERE TAMED ONCE. WE CAN CERTAINLY DO IT AGA WE ARE THE GUARDIAN OF THE UNIVERSE...

AND *YOU WILL YIELD.*

YOU WILL BE *DESTROYED.*

BOLD TALK. BUT TAMING ONE IS NOT THE SAME AS TAMING ALL, AND YOU WERE NOT THE ONES WHO HARNESSED US BEFORE. IF YOU WILL NOT STAND ASIDE...

...THAT CAN'T BE.

YES, IT CAN.

YES, IT DAMN WELL CAN.

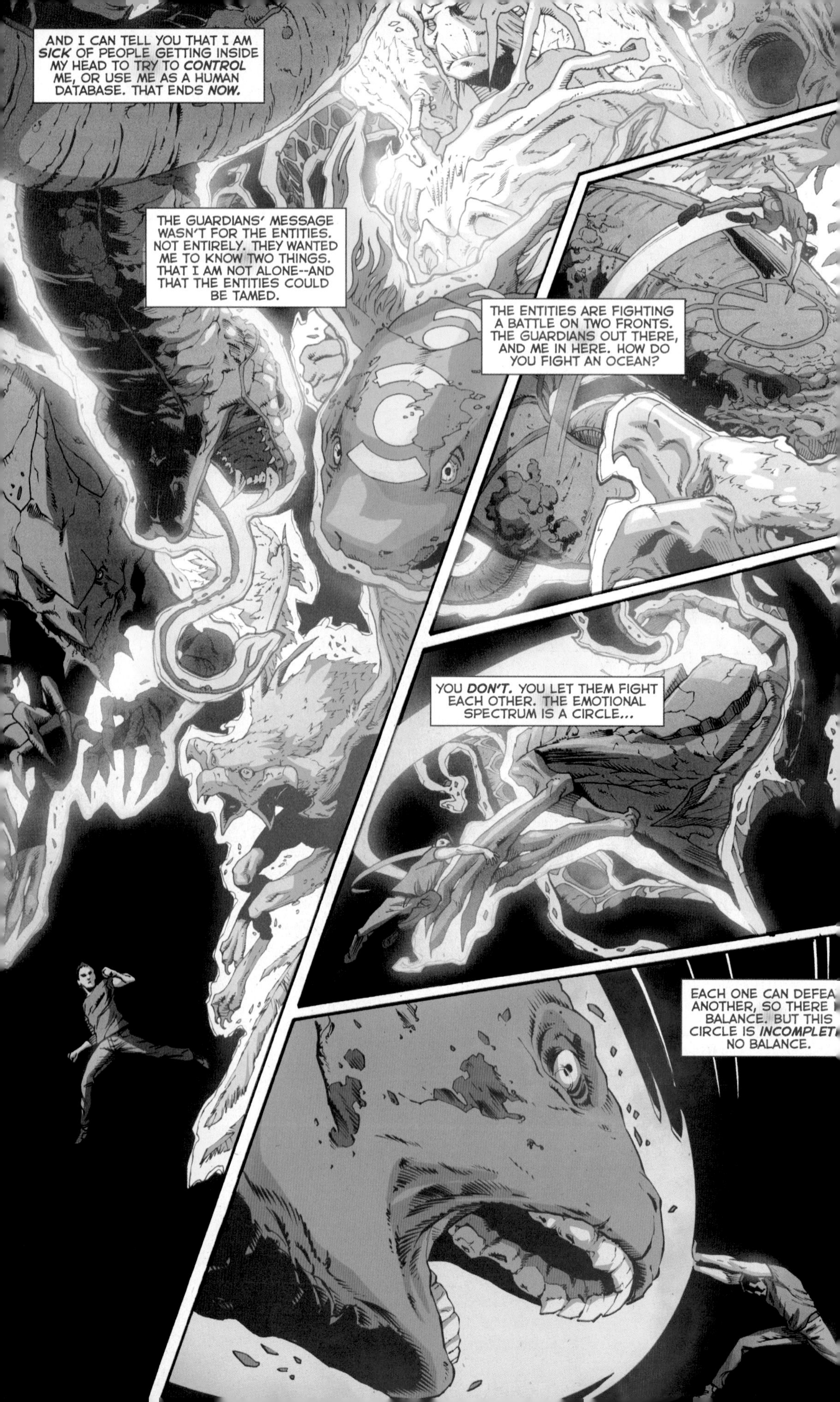
AND I CAN TELL YOU THAT I AM SICK OF PEOPLE GETTING INSIDE MY HEAD TO TRY TO CONTROL ME, OR USE ME AS A HUMAN DATABASE. THAT ENDS NOW.
THE GUARDIANS' MESSAGE WASN'T FOR THE ENTITIES. NOT ENTIRELY. THEY WANTED ME TO KNOW TWO THINGS. THAT I AM NOT ALONE--AND THAT THE ENTITIES COULD BE TAMED.
THE ENTITIES ARE FIGHTING A BATTLE ON TWO FRONTS. THE GUARDIANS OUT THERE, AND ME IN HERE. HOW DO YOU FIGHT AN OCEAN?
YOU DON'T. YOU LET THEM FIGHT EACH OTHER. THE EMOTIONAL SPECTRUM IS A CIRCLE...
EACH ONE CAN DEFEA ANOTHER, SO THERE I BALANCE. BUT THIS CIRCLE IS INCOMPLET NO BALANCE.

UNDERSTAND, LANTERN RAYNER.

AND I DO. YOU MASTER ONE EMOTION BY MASTERING ALL OF THEM. I HAVE *BALANCE.*

AND THAT IS HOW I WIN.

LANTERN RAYNER, ARE YOU... YOURSELF?

I'M IN CONTROL. THEY'RE STILL *IN* HERE, BUT I HAVE THEM CONTAINED, FOR THE MOMENT.

THAT IS A RELIEF.

YOU COULDN'T, COULD YOU?

I DO NOT UNDERSTAND, KYLE.

CONTROL THEM. NOT ALL OF THEM AT ONCE.

WE WERE PREPARED TO TRY. BUT YES, TO ANSWER THE QUESTION, WE WERE, AS YOU WOULD PUT IT, "BLUFFING."

WE SHOULD CONNECT WITH LANTERN JORDAN AND THE OTHERS AT YSMAULT. I BELIEVE HE WAS RIGHT--WITH THE ENTITIES' HELP, WE CAN DEFEAT RELIC.

NO.

I KNOW WHAT THE ENTITIES KNOW. WHAT THEY CAN FEEL. THEY ARE SCREAMING AT ME. AND I KNOW WHAT RELIC KNEW. AND HE IS RIGHT.

WE DON'T NEED TO DEFEAT RELIC...

WE NEED TO HELP HIM.

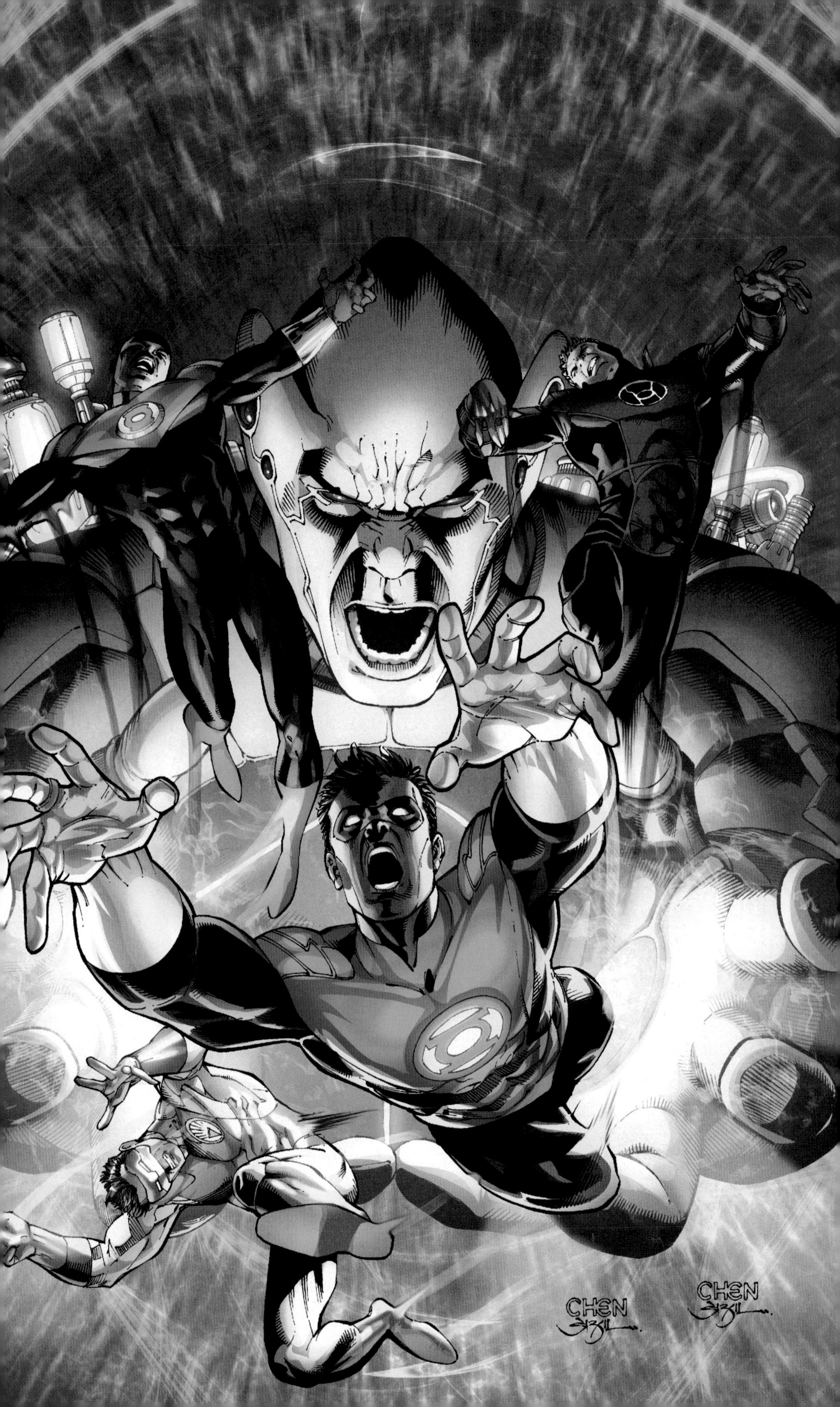

THE SOURCE
ROBERT VENDITTI writer SEAN CHEN penciller JON SIBAL & WALDEN WONG inkers
cover art by SEAN CHEN, JON SIBAL & ALEX SINCLAIR

THE UNIVERSE THAT WAS. A UNIVERSE OF BEAUTY AND WONDER.

A UNIVERSE LIKE EVERY OTHER BEFORE IT--

--FUELED BY THE POWER OF THE EMOTIONAL SPECTRUM.

DESTROYED BY THOSE WHO HARNESSED THE SPECTRUM TO MAKE WEAPONS OF LIGHT.

A SINGLE SURVIVOR. A RELIC FROM A VERSION OF CREATION LONG SINCE EXTINCT.

A SCIENTIST WHO WITNESSED WITH HORROR THE DEATH OF THAT UNIVERSE.

A BEING WHO WILL KILL--

--TO STOP THOSE WHO WOULD CAUSE IT TO HAPPEN AGAIN.

SPACE SECTOR 2814.

THE PLANET YSMAULT. HOME OF THE RED LANTERNS.

ARE WE GOING TO *DO* THIS THING OR NOT? I'VE GOT THE REDS ALL *FROTHED UP* AND READY TO *PUMMEL!*

GUY... BEFORE WE GO AFTER RELIC, THERE'S SOMETHING YOU NEED TO KNOW.

WE LOST OA, GUY.

RELIC DETONATED THE CENTRAL POWER BATTERY. THE ENTIRE *PLANET* WENT WITH IT.

JOHN... DIDN'T MAKE IT.

RED LANTERN RAGE
BIG-TIME RAGE

WHAT?!

GREEN LANTERN WILL

THE GREEN LANTERN I *BROKE SKULLS* WITH. MY *BEST FRIEND.*

YOU *LET HIM DIE?*

I DIDN'T *LET* HIM DO ANYTHING. HE VOLUNTEERED.

OUR RINGS ARE ON *FUMES,* AND WE DON'T HAVE ANY WAY TO RECHARGE.

JOHN TOOK A HANDFUL OF RECRUITS AND WENT *HEAD TO HEAD* WITH RELIC, SO THE REST OF US COULD ESCAPE.

WHERE IS THIS *RELIC?* I'LL TEAR OUT HIS THROAT AND *STRANGLE* HIM WITH IT!

THAT'S THE PROBLEM. WE THINK KYLE IS WITH HIM, BUT HIS RING IS BEING MASKED SOMEHOW. WE DON'T KNOW WHERE THEY ARE.

STAR SAPHIRE LOVE

I MIGHT...

...KNOW WHERE KYLE IS. MAYBE.

NO, ACTUALLY, I DO. I KNOW WHERE HE IS.

CAROL? HOW DO *YOU* KNOW WHERE KYLE IS?

DID HE TELL YOU WHERE HE WAS HEADED?

NOT EXACTLY. I JUST SORT OF... *FEEL* IT.

YOU... YOU'RE A STAR SAPPHIRE. YOUR RING IS POWERED BY *LOVE.*

AND YOU CAN FEEL WHERE *KYLE* IS?

AWKWARD.

NOW I SEE WHY YOU ENDED THINGS BETWEEN US. YOU GAVE A WHOLE SPEECH ABOUT ME NEEDING TO *GROW UP,* BUT WHAT YOU *REALLY* WANT IS KYLE!

SPEAKING OF GROWING UP, CAN YOU NOT DO THIS WHILE THE *FATE* OF *EVERY LANTERN* HANGS IN THE BALANCE?

...FAIR ENOUGH.

THANK YOU.

NOW GIVE ME SPACE, SO I CAN SEND OUT A TETHER.

ADVANCE WARNING, EVERYONE.

"I HAVE *NO IDEA* WHAT'S WAITING FOR US ON THE OTHER SIDE."

BORDER OF THE UNIVERSE.

EMITTING SPECTRUM ENERGIES.

BEGINNING STRUCTURE ANALYSIS.

ANALYSIS NOT POSSI-KKRT-

KKRRK

THE PROBES ARE *STILL* INADEQUATE.

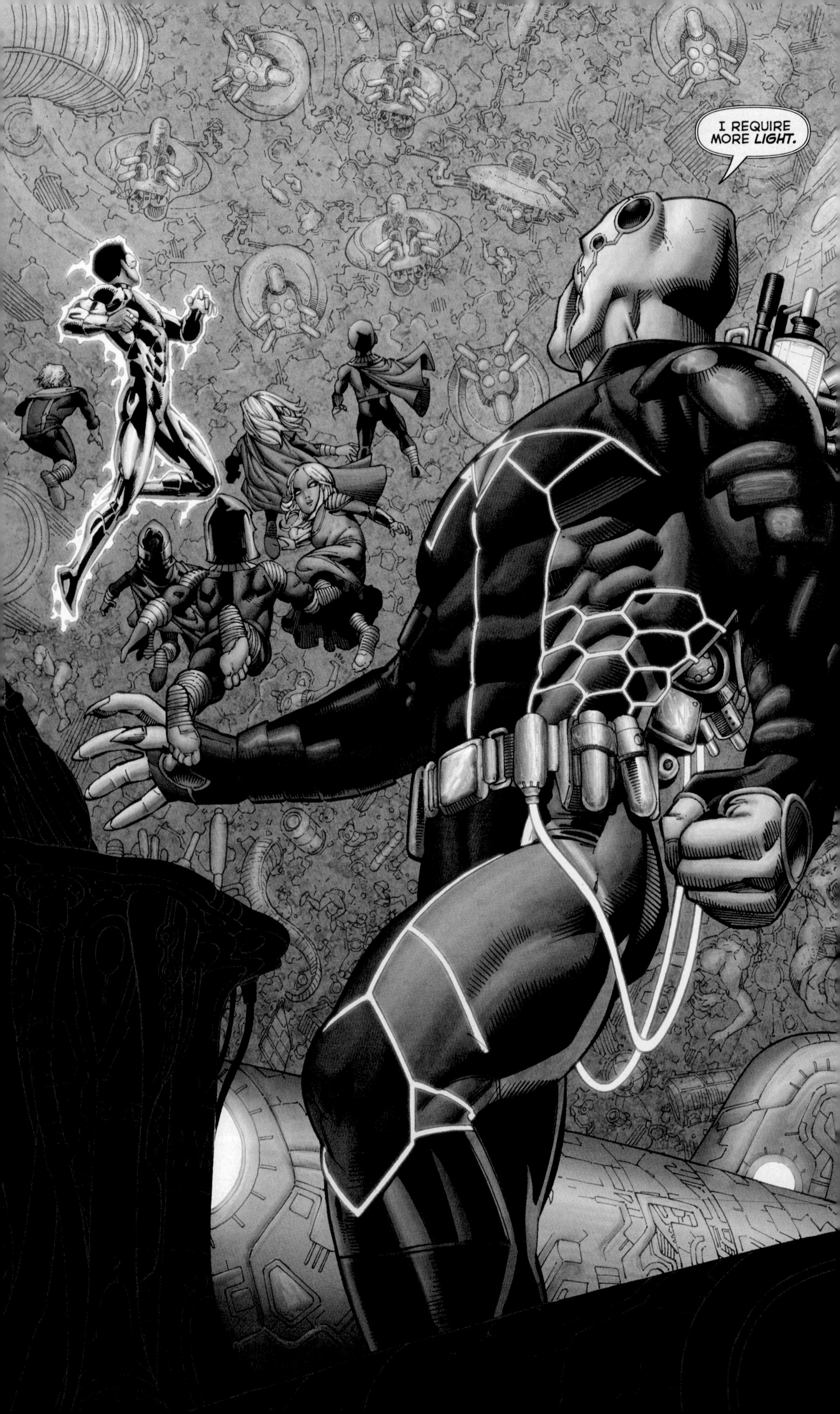
I REQUIRE MORE *LIGHT*.

WE GUARDIANS ARE ETERNAL BEINGS, RELIC. BELIEVE US WHEN WE SAY THE *SOURCE WALL* IS *IMPASSABLE.*

IT ENCIRCLES THE UNIVERSE IN EVERY DIRECTION. IT CAN NEITHER BE CIRCUMVENTED NOR BREACHED.

INDEED, IT IS ENCRUSTED WITH THE CALCIFIED REMAINS OF EVERYTHING THAT HAS TRIED TO GRASP ITS MYSTERIES.

IT WAS THE SAME IN MY UNIVERSE. THAT'S THE REASON I'M *CERTAIN* THE SOURCE LIES BEYOND.

WHEN *YOU* SPEAK OF "THE SOURCE," YOU MEAN--

THE RESERVOIR FOR THE EMOTIONAL SPECTRUM. THE FONT FROM WHICH ALL EMOTION FLOWS INTO THE UNIVERSE, POWERING CREATION.

THE *SOURCE.* WHICH YOUR GREEN LIGHTSMITHS--LIGHTSMITHS OF *EVERY* HUE--HAVE RECKLESSLY DEPLETED.

IF WE'RE TO RETURN TO IT THE LIGHT I'VE CAPTURED, WE MUST FIRST REACH IT.

THE ENTITIES INSIDE ME AGREE WITH YOU. THEY AREN'T SURE WHAT HAPPENS NEXT, BUT THEY KNOW WE *HAVE* TO REFILL THE RESERVOIR.

WHY IT TOOK THE ENTITIES AND A GUY FROM A *DEAD UNIVERSE* TO MAKE ME REALIZE THE ENERGY OUR RINGS USE ISN'T INFINITE, I HAVE NO IDEA.

IN MY DEFENSE, I *AM* HUMAN.

BUT WHAT'S YOUR EXCUSE, PAALKO? AND I DON'T WANT TO HEAR ABOUT HOW YOU WERE IN ISOLATION FOR A FEW *BILLION* YEARS.

ISN'T THERE ANY MENTION OF THE RESERVOIR IN THE BOOK OF OA?

THE BOOK OF OA DOES NOT TELL THE COMPLETE STORY. LIKE ANY CHRONICLE OF HISTORY, IT WAS WRITTEN BY THOSE WITH AN AGENDA.

AS A *HUMAN,* LANTERN RAYNER, I WOULD EXPECT YOU TO UNDERSTAND *THAT* AS WELL.

THE WHITE LANTERN 2LIFE

WHAT IF THE ENTITIES WERE WRONG TO LEAD ME HERE? WHAT IF THE RESERVOIR *ISN'T* ON THE OTHER SIDE OF THE WALL?

IT COULD BE ON A PLANET SOMEWHERE, OR INSIDE A QUASAR, OR--

NO!

I DEDICATED MY EXISTENCE TO FINDING MY UNIVERSE'S RESERVOIR. DISPATCHED PROBES TO COUNTLESS STARS AND WORLDS. TRAVELED TO EVERY CORNER.

ALL MY SEARCHES ENDED AT THE WALL.

RELEASE US!

THE RESERVOIR *IS* BEYOND THE WALL. IT MUST BE.

I WAS SURE I'D CAPTURED ENOUGH SPECTRUM ENERGY TO PIERCE IT, BUT PERHAPS YOU CAN GIVE ME WHAT I NEED.

STOP! WE WANT TO *HELP* YOU!

A *WHITE* LIGHTSMITH.

MY UNIVERSE POSSESSED NO SUCH THING. I DON'T YET UNDERSTAND WHAT MAKES YOU WHAT YOU ARE. I ONLY HOPE IT'S USEFUL.

AS SHOULD YOU. IF THE RESERVOIR ISN'T REPLENISHED, EVERYTHING WILL END.

DON'T!

I TRIED TO REASON WITH THE LIGHTSMITHS OF MY UNIVERSE. BEGGED THEM TO RELINQUISH THE LIGHT. THEY REFUSED.

I'LL NOT MAKE THAT MISTAKE AGAIN. VIOLENCE IS THE ONLY ARGUMENT YOUR KIND UNDERSTANDS. SO WITH VIOLENCE I WILL *SHOW* YOU.

GET THEM--

GET THEM OFF!

I ACCEPT YOUR OFFER OF HELP.

DRAIN COMMENCED.

POWER LEVEL 73%.

POWER LEVEL 59%.

FZZASSSH

RESIST, LANTERN RAYNER. WITHOUT YOU, *LIFE* WILL BE NO MORE.

FEEL THE AVARICE--

--FOR EVERYTHING YOU LOVE.

LET YOUR SUFFERING BE AN ACT OF COMPASSION.

AND BE UNAFRAID. YOU ARE THE KEY. ONLY YOU CAN TAKE US HOME.

FAIL, AND ALL HOPE IS LOST.

BRILLIANT...

THE EMOTIONAL SPECTRUM IN LIVING FORM! OF COURSE!

COULD YOU *LIGHTBEASTS* HARBOR THE SPECTRUM ENERGY I SEEK?

DO NOT HARM THEM!

TO TAMPER WITH THE ENTITIES IS TO TAMPER WITH REALITY ITSELF!

NOT TAMPER. EXPERIMENT.

EXTRACTING.

HNNGAHHHH!

KSSHH

HEY! *GULLIVER!*

THAT BUTTERFLY YOU'RE PULLING THE WINGS OFF OF?

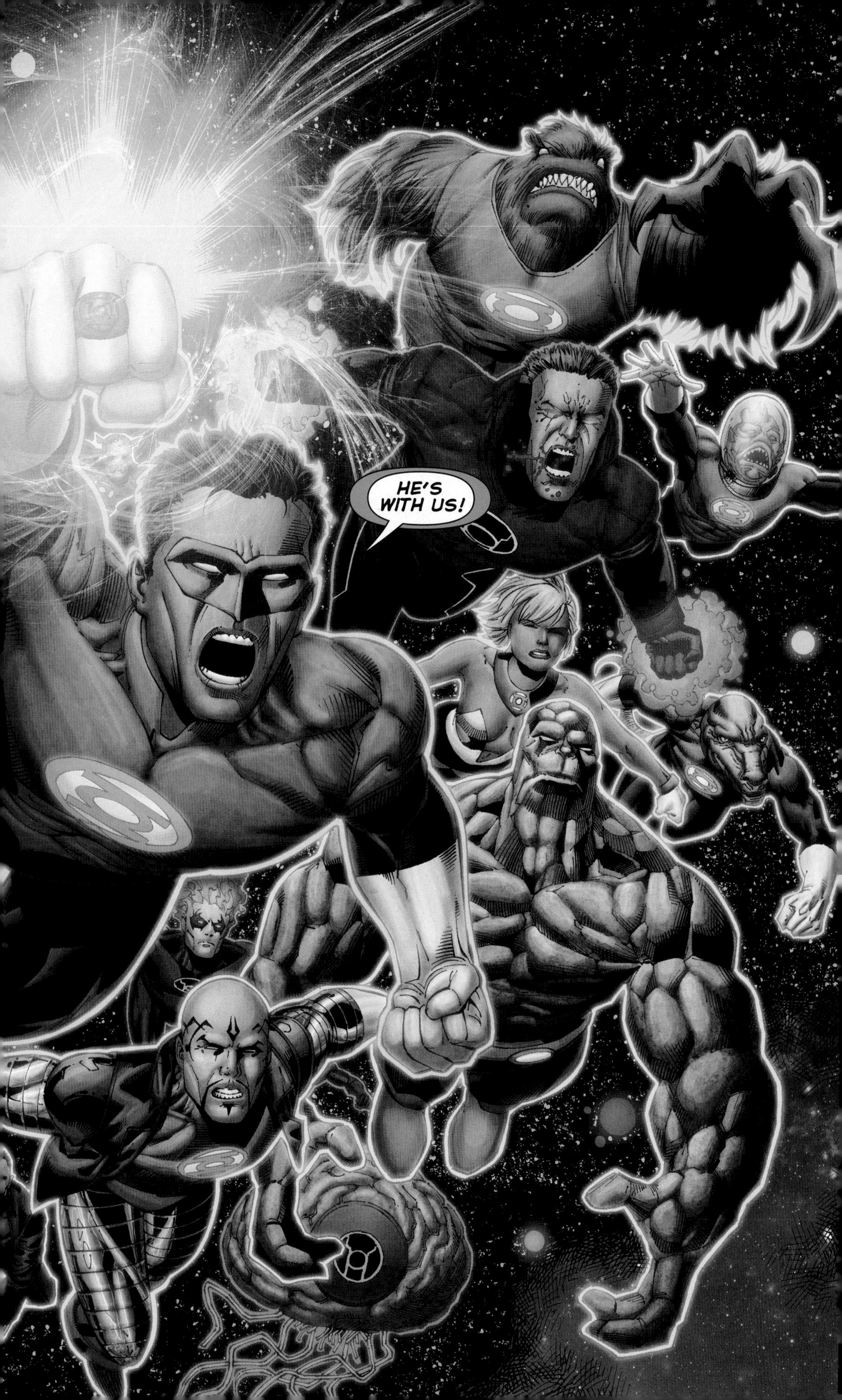
HE'S WITH US!

THEN YOU CAN *EXPIRE* WITH HIM!

AUTOMATED DEFENSES ACTIVATED.

SSKKRROON

SSKKRROON

SSKKRROON

LANTERNS, IF THERE WAS EVER A TIME TO *SHINE*--

--IT'S *NOW!*

"NO FEAR!"

SPACE SECTOR 2814.

HOME OF THE INDIGO TRIBE. THE PLANET NOK.

RING, SCOUR THE UNIVERSE. FIND THE HIGHEST CONCENTRATION OF GREEN ENERGY. THAT'S WHERE THE CORPS WILL BE.

GREEN ENERGY LOCATED.

LANTERN STEWART? IS IT TIME TO GO?

IT IS FOR ME, TWO-SIX. MY PLACE IS WITH THE REST OF THE CORPS.

BUT YOU ROOKIES HAVE BEEN THROUGH ENOUGH. I'VE NO RIGHT TO ASK ANY MORE OF YOU.

I'M NOT EVEN SURE WHAT DIFFERENCE YOU COULD MAKE.

IF MY MATH IS CORRECT--AND IT ALWAYS IS--THE ODDS ARE WORSE THAN ANYONE THINKS.

THAT ISN'T OUR FOCUS, THOUGH. WE HAVEN'T EARNED OUR EMBLEMS YET, BUT WE'RE STILL GREEN LANTERNS.

LONG ODDS ARE WHAT WE *DO*, RIGHT?

KEEP TALKING LIKE THAT, FESKA, AND YOU'LL HAVE YOUR EMBLEMS SOON ENOUGH.

YOU STOOD WITH THE INDIGO TRIBE ONCE, LANTERN STEWART. NOW WE STAND WITH YOU.

INDIGO TRIBE COMPASSION

NOK.

TO THE LAST.

I'LL TAKE EVERY EXTRA HAND YOU CAN SPARE, NATROMO.

I NEED MORE THAN YOUR TRIBE, THOUGH. I NEED YOUR *EXPERTISE*.

HOW ABOUT IT, OLD MAN?

YOU READY TO *BUILD?*

LOOK HOW YOU *SQUANDER* LIGHT!

DO YOU NOT UNDERSTAND THERE MUST BE A COST?

YOU'RE THE BABYSITTER WHO LETS THE KIDS JUMP OFF THE *ROOF* INTO THE POOL.

RELIC HAS TAKEN MORE FROM ME THAN ANYONE. HE'S A *MADMAN*, BUT THAT DOESN'T MAKE HIM *WRONG*.

WATCH MY BACK WHILE I CUT YOUR *MAN* FREE.

LET IT *GO*, HAL!

SOMETHING *IS* HAPPENING, HAL. TO THE ENTITIES. TO THE EMOTIONAL SPECTRUM.

YOU JUST WON'T SEE IT.

I'LL BE SURE TO TAKE A GOOD, *LONG* LOOK.

POWER LEVEL 8%.

I GAVE YOU A MISSION, KYLE. KEEP THE GUARDIANS *OUT* OF TROUBLE, NOT *LEAD* THEM TO IT.

AFTER I MAKE SURE NO MORE LANTERNS GET KILLED.

HEY, TALL, PALE, AND UGLY! EVER TANGLED WITH THE CHARM CITY P.D.?

CAPTURING SPECTRUM ENERGY.

FOOLISH LIGHTSMITH.

REDIRECTING.

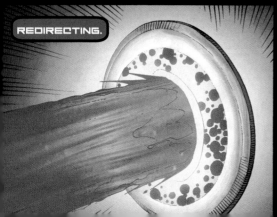

OOPS.

RELIC KNOWS HOW TO SEND LIGHT RIGHT BACK AT US. HE AND HIS SHIP ARE PROTECTED.

JOHN! I THOUGHT YOU DIED, OLD BUDDY!

MAN, AM I *GLAD* TO--

MOVE!

--TELL YOUR *PARTNER* WHY YOU QUIT THE CORPS AND SWITCHED TO THE REDS?

KRACK

WE'LL CONTINUE THIS *CONVERSATION* LATER.

THE NEW UNIFORM MAKES YOU LOOK LIKE A *DERANGED SANTA,* BY THE WAY.

HEH.

RED LANTERNS! TEAR THE SHIP APART! NO LIGHT!

"ONLY RAGE!"

DEFENSIVE POSITIONS, ROOKIES! GIVE THE REDS SPACE TO DO THEIR WORST!

CONSERVE AS MUCH CHARGE AS YOU CAN!

NO OPPONENT IS TOO LARGE FOR JRUK!

WE'RE SUPPOSED TO BE ON DEFENSE, JRUK. *DEFENSE.*

LET HIM GO. HE'S ENJOYING HIMSELF.

BOOOM

KRMMBBLL

MY SHIP... ALL THE LIGHT I PRESERVED...

NO!

KKRRRKKKRRKK

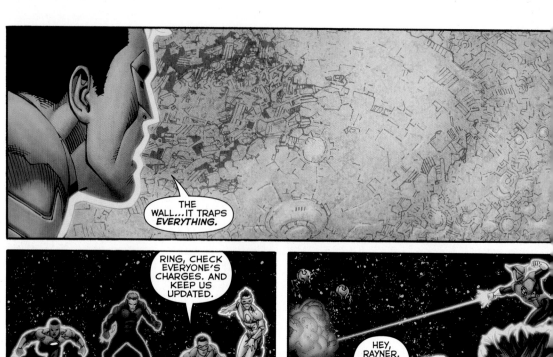

THE WALL...IT TRAPS *EVERYTHING.*

RING, CHECK EVERYONE'S CHARGES. AND KEEP US UPDATED.

POWER LEVEL 5%.

POWER LEVEL 12%.

POWER LEVEL 6%.

POWER LEVEL 28%.

HEY, RAYNER. GET IN THE FIGHT, WHY DON'T YOU?

KYLE ASIDE, WE'VE GOT ENOUGH POWER FOR *ONE MORE* RUN. BUT WE CAN'T WASTE OUR CHARGES ON BLASTS OR CONSTRUCTS.

SO, YOU GUYS READY FOR A GAME OF GOOD OLD-FASHIONED *CHICKEN?*

INDIGO-1, CAN YOU TELEPORT US BETWEEN RELIC AND HIS REFLECTORS-- AND *KEEP* US THERE?

NOK.

YOU'VE SEEN THAT SPECTRUM WEAPONS ARE *USELESS* AGAINST ME.

YET STILL YOU WASTE LIGHT.

IT'S NO MYSTERY WHY YOUR UNIVERSE IS ABOUT TO DIE.

YOU KEEP SAYING YOU'RE TRYING TO SAVE US, RELIC. PROBLEM IS, YOU'RE *KILLING* US WHILE YOU SAY IT.

FACING ME ALONE WILL BRING DEATH TO *YOU* MORE SWIFTLY, LIGHTSMITH.

TOO BAD FOR YOU, HE *ISN'T* ALONE.

AND I'VE TOLD YOU ALREADY--

--WE'RE LANTERNS!

YOU ARE AGENTS OF *DECAY!*

GYARRG!

YOU WANT TO SEE DECAY? GUY, SHOW HIM DECAY!

WHAM

GHNN

NOK.

RARRRGH!

DRIVE HIM INTO THE WALL!

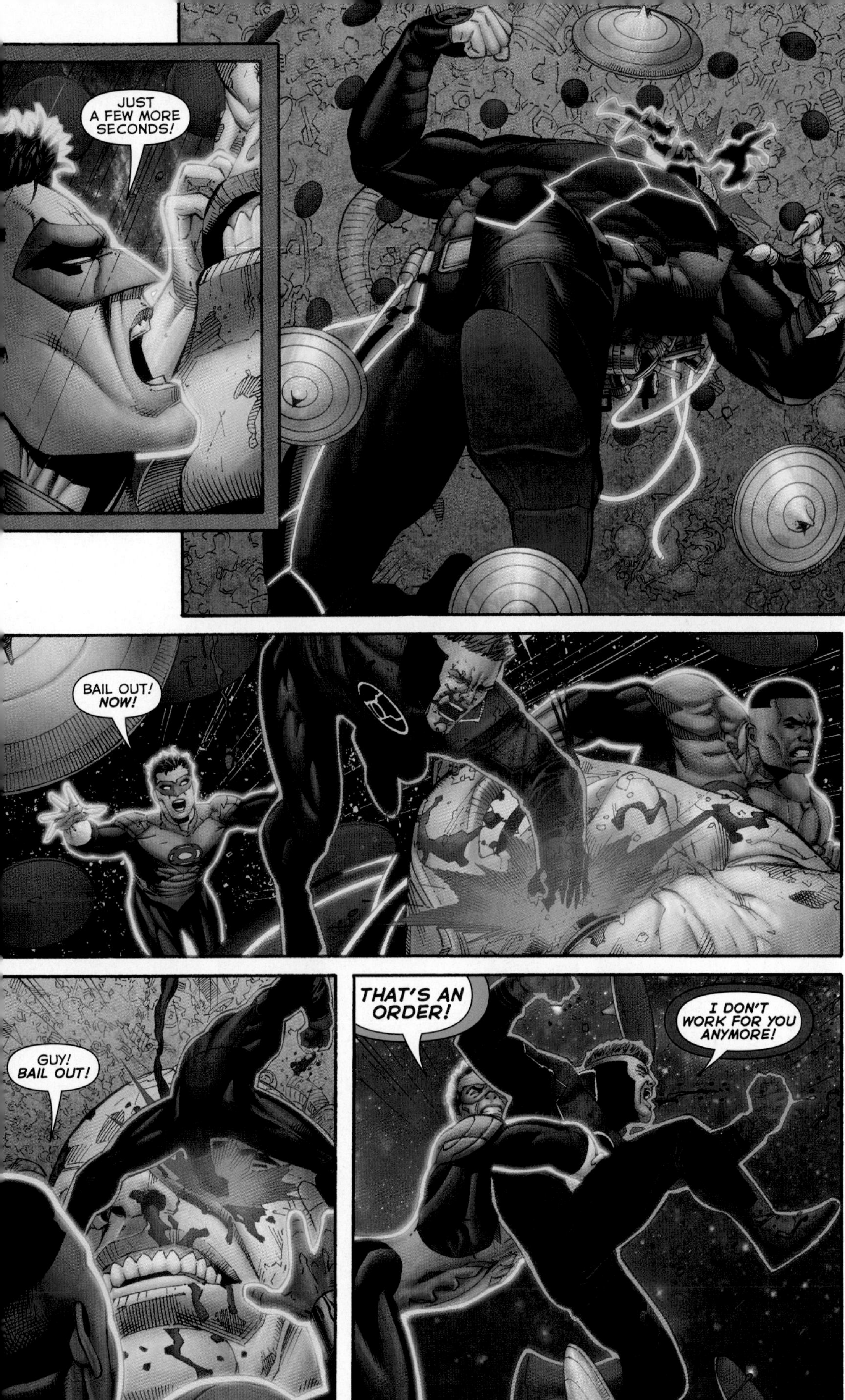
JUST A FEW MORE SECONDS!
BAIL OUT! NOW!
GUY! BAIL OUT!
THAT'S AN ORDER!
I DON'T WORK FOR YOU ANYMORE!

YOU JUST CAN'T LET *ME* WIN, CAN YOU?

YOU WERE GETTING TOO CLOSE TO THE WALL! YOU WANT TO GET STUCK HERE FOR *ETERNITY*?

WHERE'S KYLE?

IT'S JUST YOU AND ME, RELIC.

POWER LEVEL 14%.

IGNORANT FOOL! I ONLY WISH TO SAVE YOUR UNIVERSE!

GET OUT OF THERE!

KYLE!

YOU WANT TO UNLOCK THE MYSTERY OF THE SOURCE WALL? GOOD. WE'RE BOTH ABOUT TO STUDY IT *UP CLOSE.*

POWER LEVEL 20%.

YOU SEE? THE WALL CRUMBLES. BLACKNESS POURS OUT. THE RESERVOIR IS *DEPLETED.*

WITNESS, LITTLE LIGHTSMITH. WITNESS THE END OF CREATION.

YOUR GOALS MAY BE NOBLE, RELIC, BUT YOUR METHODS *SUCK.*

POWER LEVEL 33%.

I SURVIVED AN END ALREADY. I WILL AGAIN.

I'LL KEEP RETURNING UNTIL I STOP THE LIGHTSMITHS' CYCLE OF DESTRUCTION. IT'S MY CALLING.

CALLING. THAT'S A GOOD WAY TO PUT IT.

POWER LEVEL 52%.

I HAVE ONE, TOO. THE MORE I EMBRACE LIFE-- THE MORE I FIGHT FOR IT--THE *STRONGER* I GET.

I DIDN'T UNDERSTAND WHAT THAT MEANT, UNTIL NOW.

POWER LEVEL 74%.

YOU AREN'T THE KEY, RELIC. I AM.

POWER LEVEL 99%.

100% POWER REACHED.

BEAUTIFUL...

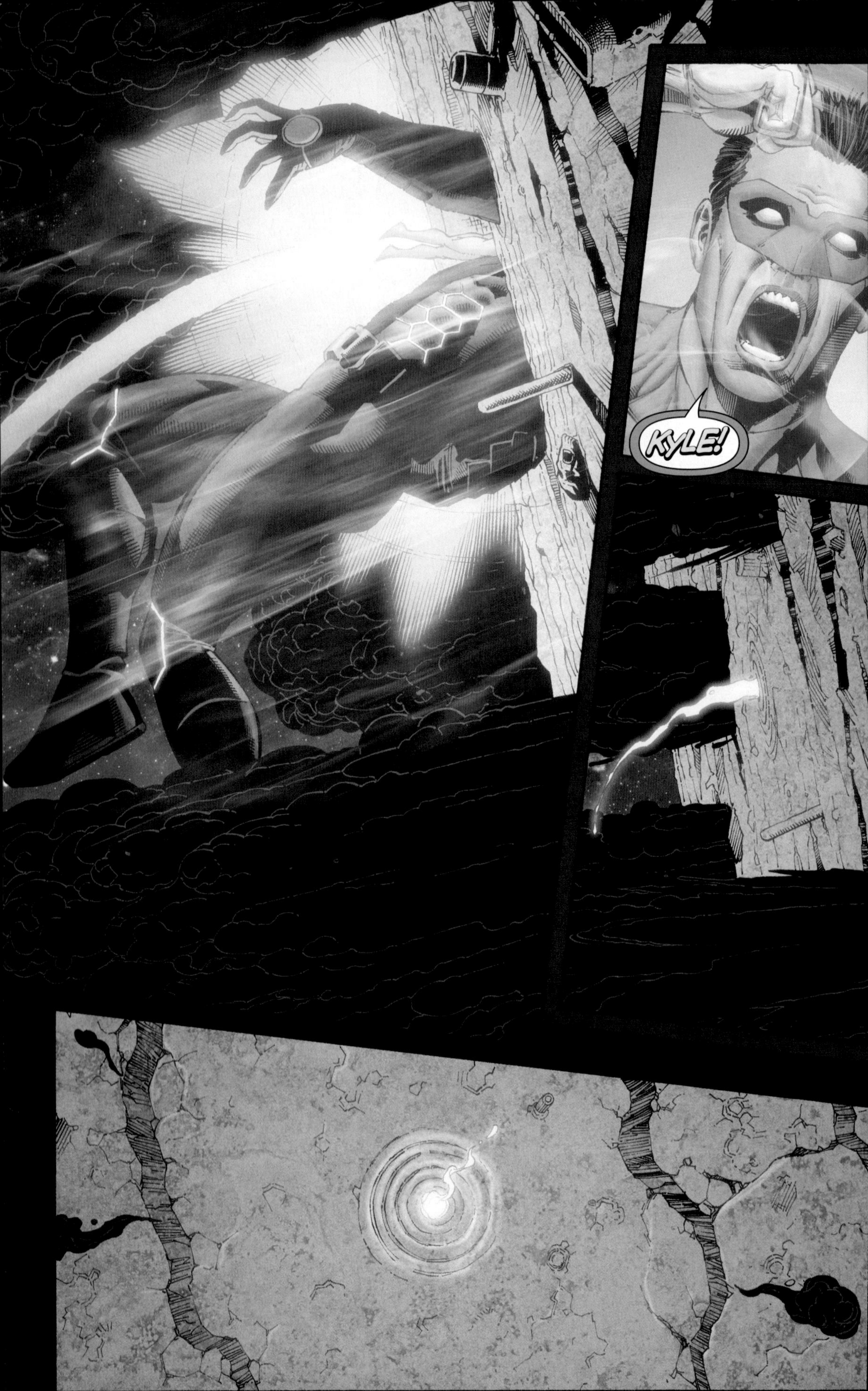
KYLE!

FWASH!

LOOK, BROTHERS AND SISTERS!

"THE WHITE LANTERN *RETURNS!*"

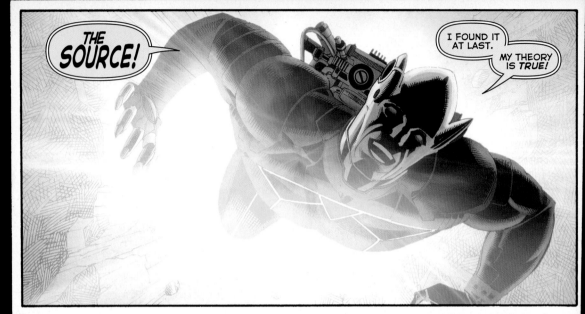

THE SOURCE!

I FOUND IT AT LAST.

MY THEORY IS *TRUE!*

THE RESERVOIR HAS BEEN REPLENISHED.

THE *WHITE LIGHTSMITH* WAS THE SOLUTION!

RESPECT THE OPPORTUNITY YOU'VE BEEN GIVEN.

MY WORK... IS FINISHED.

RRRRKRRKKRRRKK

DMFLLN NNNG

KYLE...

HE'S... GONE.

HE WENT DOWN IN THE LINE OF DUTY, AND WE'LL ALL HONOR HIM FOR IT. BUT RIGHT NOW YOU NEED TO GET EVERYONE ELSE TO SAFETY.

HOW? JOHN IS TAPPED, AND THE REST OF US AREN'T FAR BEHIND.

I LED THE CORPS HERE, AND WE BEAT RELIC, BUT FOR WHAT? NONE OF US ARE GOING HOME.

POWER LEVEL 2%.

POWER LEVEL 0%.

POWER LEVEL 4%.

DON'T COUNT ON THE REDS FOR HELP. THEY HEAR YOU GREENS ARE OUT OF JUICE, THEY'LL BITE YOUR HEADS OFF.

MINE, TOO, IF I TRY TO STOP THEM. IT'S KIND OF AN ONLY-THE-BRUTAL-SURVIVE OUTFIT.

HAL, I...

GO ON, CAROL. GET YOURSELF TO AN ATMOSPHERE.

I DON'T WANT YOU TO SEE WHAT HAPPENS.

POWER LEVEL 1%.

FOR CRYING OUT LOUD. YOU MAY BE CORPS LEADER, HAL, BUT NOT EVERYTHING RESTS ON YOUR SHOULDERS.

I'VE ALREADY ARRANGED A TICKET HOME WITH THE INDIGOS.

WE WILL REMAIN HERE, LANTERN STEWART. LANTERN RAYNER'S PASSING MUST BE MOURNED.

HONOR HIM FOR ALL OF US.

INDIGO-1, DOES YOUR TRIBE HAVE ENOUGH CHARGE TO TELEPORT US ALL AWAY?

...NOK?

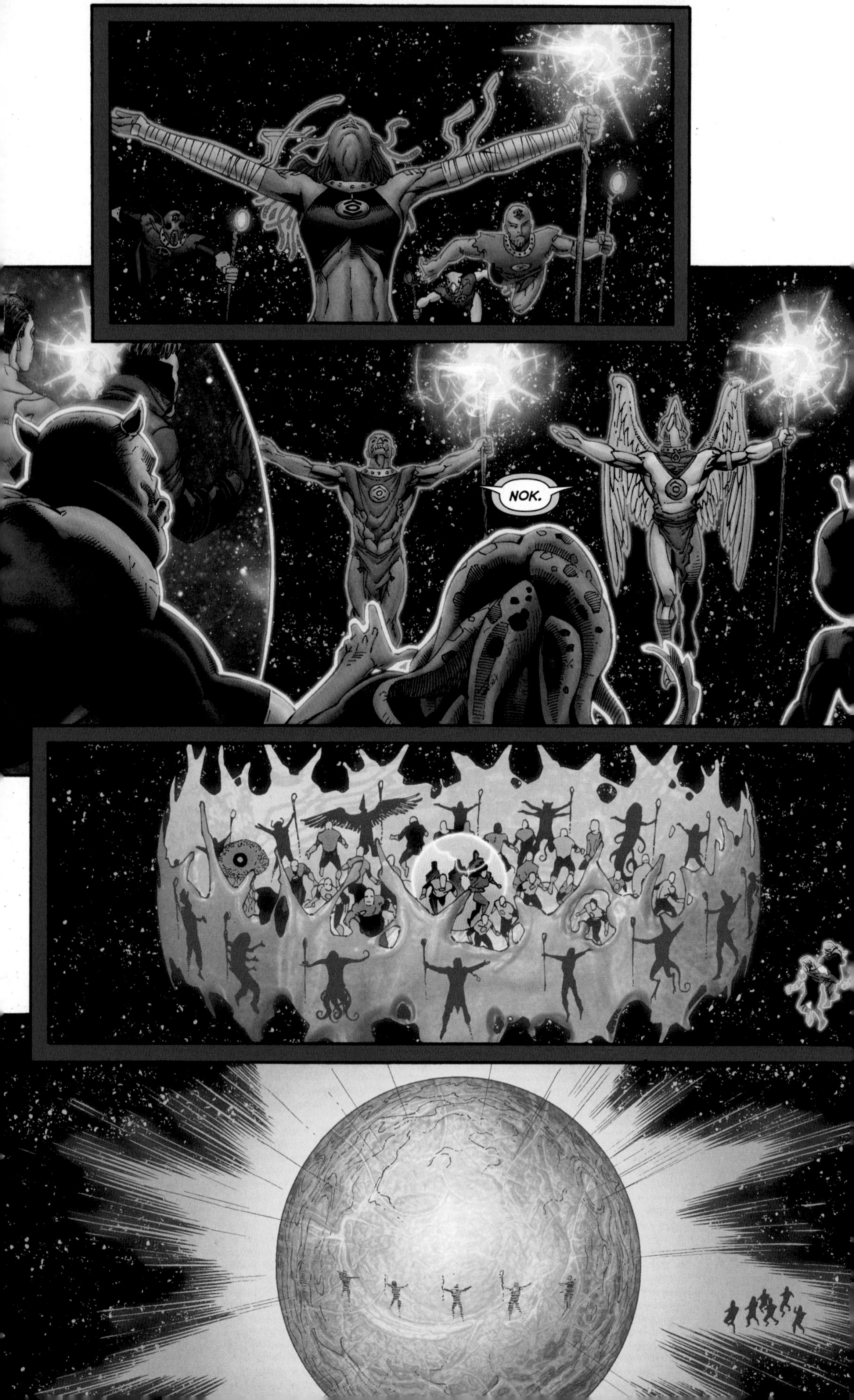
NOK.

POWER LEVEL 0%.

WHERE ARE WE?

WAIT. IS THIS...?

WELCOME, CORPS LEADER JORDAN.

WELCOME TO THE NEW HOME OF THE GREEN LANTERN CORPS.

SPACE SECTOR ZERO
THE SENTIENT PLANET MOGO

A *NEW* CENTRAL POWER BATTERY? ...*HOW?*

IT WAS MY CALL. AFTER RELIC DESTROYED OA, I WENT TO THE INDIGO TRIBE FOR HELP.

YOU ONCE SAW ME RESTORE A BATTERY, LANTERN JORDAN. ALL I REQUIRE IS THE PIECES.

MOGO ISOLATED THE DUST OF YOUR BATTERY AMONG THE DEBRIS OF YOUR FORMER PLANET...AND SUPPLIED THE SPARK OF GREEN LIGHT NEEDED TO REKINDLE IT.

NOT BAD, NATROMO. NOT BAD AT ALL.

DON'T SUPPOSE YOU WANT TO TEACH *ME* HOW TO BUILD ONE?

ANYONE HAVE EYES ON GUY?

ISSEK LOREK YSMAULT LOK.

THE RED LANTERNS WERE TELEPORTED TO THEIR *OWN* WORLD. WAS THIS NOT CORRECT?

HE'S BACK ON *YSMAULT?*

STRANDED BEHIND ENEMY LINES...

WE'LL GET HIM BACK, JOHN. IT'S MY MESS. I'LL FIND A WAY TO CLEAN IT UP.

WE'VE BEEN THROUGH DARK DAYS, LANTERNS.

OUR HOME WAS DESTROYED. WE LOST SOME OF OUR *BEST.*

LANTERNS WE CALLED FRIENDS. LANTERNS LIKE *KYLE RAYNER,* WHO DEDICATED HIS *LIFE* TO SERVING THE CORPS.

BUT WE OVERCAME IT ALL.

FROM VETERAN TO RECRUIT, YOU FOUGHT AS ONE. YOU GAVE NEW MEANING TO THE PHRASE *"NO FEAR."*

NOW WE'RE GOING TO LAY A NEW FOUNDATION RIGHT HERE. THE GREEN LANTERN CORPS WILL BE *STRONGER* AND MORE *JUST* THAN EVER BEFORE.

OUR *LIGHT* WILL *SHINE* IN EVERY CORNER OF THE UNIVERSE. SO *CHARGE UP AND LET ME HEAR IT!*

IN BRIGHTEST DAY, IN BLACKEST NIGHT--

NO EVIL SHALL ESCAPE OUR SIGHT!

LET THOSE WHO WORSHIP EVIL'S MIGHT--

BEWARE OUR POWER...

GREEN LANTERN'S... LIGHT?

GRAF? YOU'RE A LIGHT MONK. I KNOW *YOU* HAVEN'T FORGOTTEN THE OATH...

I CANNOT RECITE IT, HAL. NOT ANYMORE.

ME NEITHER.

NOR I.

WHY? WHAT'S THE MATTER WITH YOU?

DON'T YOU SEE? RELIC WAS RIGHT. WIELDING THE LIGHT *DOES* DEPLETE THE RESERVOIR OF THE EMOTIONAL SPECTRUM.

THE CLOCK IS ALREADY WINDING DOWN ON THE UNIVERSE'S SECOND LIFE. WE WON'T BE A PARTY TO SPEEDING IT UP.

KYLE MAY HAVE REPLENISHED THE RESERVOIR *THIS* TIME, BUT HE'S *GONE*...

"WHO CAN SAY IF THERE WILL EVER BE ANOTHER *WHITE LANTERN?*"

LANTERN RAYNER'S DEATH IS A GREAT LOSS.

HE WAS A TRULY UNIQUE BEING. THERE IS SO MUCH MORE HE MIGHT HAVE TAUGHT US. AND WE, HIM.

HOW WAS HE ABLE TO PASS BEYOND THE WALL, PAALKO? HAVE YOU EVER HEARD OF SUCH A THING?

NOT IN ALL MY EONS. MORE INTRIGUING STILL...WHAT WAITS TO BE DISCOVERED ON THE OTHER SIDE?

WE DEPARTED OA TO LEARN ABOUT THE UNIVERSE. IS THERE A GREATER QUESTION THAN THIS?

?

MUST YOU POKE *EVERYTHING* WITH A STICK?

I DID NOT TOUCH IT, ZALLA! I ONLY *ALMOST* DID!

FWASH

FWASHHH

COULD IT BE...?

NYAAGH!

LANTERN RAYNER!

UHNNHN.

WHAT OCCURRED? TELL US!

THE ENTITIES... THEY SACRIFICED THEMSELVES. THEY SAID IT WAS THE ONLY WAY TO REFILL THE RESERVOIR.

THEY'RE... DEAD.

WHAT ELSE, LANTERN RAYNER?

ALL YOU WITNESSED. ALL YOU EXPERIENCED. WE MUST KNOW EVERYTHING!

I... I CAN'T REMEMBER.

GNYAA!

YOU *CANNOT*, OR YOU *DO* NOT? PERHAPS I CAN AID YOU.

BROTHER? WHAT DID YOU SEE?

NO ONE CAN KNOW...

THE UNIVERSE HAS BEEN GRANTED A NEW BEGINNING, MY FELLOW GUARDIANS. WE WILL HONOR THIS GIFT BY REDEDICATING OURSELVES TO THE PURSUIT OF LEARNING.

BUT *ABOVE ALL*, LANTERN RAYNER'S RETURN MUST REMAIN A *SECRET*.

IT IS TIME HIS JOURNEY *TRULY* BEGAN.

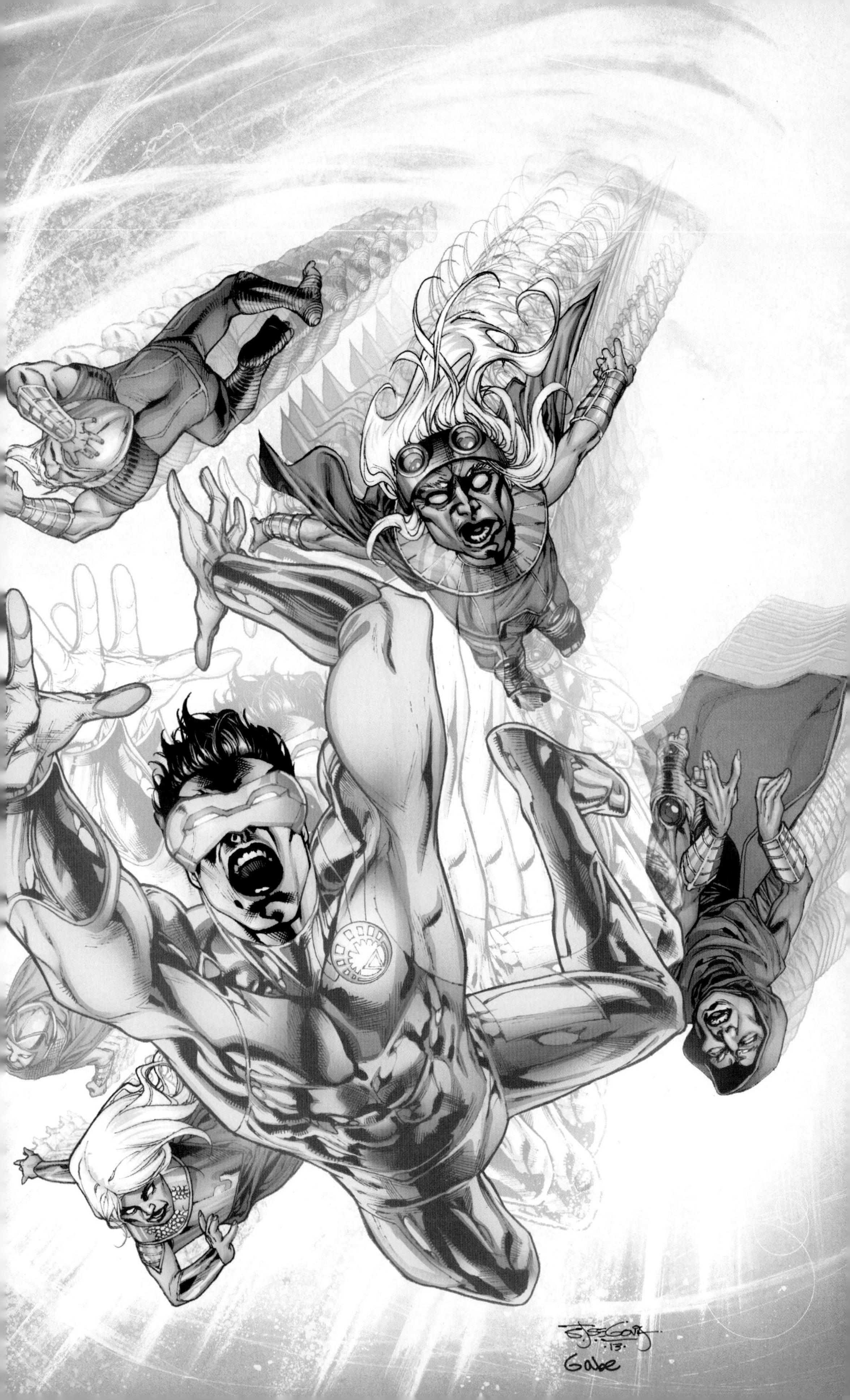
Gabe

ALL TOMORROW'S PARTIES
JUSTIN JORDAN writer BRAD WALKER & GERALDO BORGES pencillers
ANDREW HENNESSY & CAM SMITH inkers cover art by STEPHEN JORGE SEGOVIA & GABE ELTAEB

SPACE SECTOR 1416.

ZAMARON. HOMEWORLD OF THE STAR SAPPHIRES.

"ARE WE BEING *THREATENED*, CAROL FERRIS?"

NO. FOR ALL HIS TOUGH TALK ABOUT "POLICING THE RINGS," I REALLY DON'T THINK HAL JORDAN IS A THREAT. *YET.* BUT HE'S RIGHT ABOUT ONE THING.

WE SACRIFICED A LOT TO KEEP THESE RINGS. OA, THE BLUE LANTERNS... *KYLE...*

THIS POWER IS A *GIFT*, AND WE NEED TO THINK LONG AND HARD ABOUT HOW WE USE IT.

ARE YOU IMPLYING YOU ARE UNHAPPY WITH OUR COMMAND?

I'M NOT *IMPLYING* ANYTHING. I AM *SAYING* THAT I THINK THE STAR SAPPHIRES CAN DO BETTER THAN WE'VE DONE. AND THAT WE *OWE* IT TO THOSE WHO GAVE THEIR LIVES FOR US.

WE ARE AWARE OF LANTERN RAYNER'S SACRIFICE, CAROL. AND WE *ARE* GRATEFUL. BUT YOU ARE NOT IN CHARGE. IT IS *OUR* DUTY TO--

HOLD ON, I'M GETTING A CALL.

...PARDON?

SORRY.

I HAVE TO GO.

I NEED TO SEE ABOUT A...

JERK!

OW. AND, UH... WHAT?

YOU LET ME-- LET *ALL* OF US-- THINK YOU WERE *DEAD,* KYLE. WHY DIDN'T YOU *TELL* ME YOU WERE ALIVE?!

I *DID* TELL YOU I WAS ALIVE! THAT'S WHY YOU'RE *HERE!*

NO, THE *GUARDIANS* ASKED ME TO COME TO... *WHEREVER* THE HECK THIS PLACE IS, TO--

--AND I AM QUOTING HERE--

--"ADDRESS A MATTER OF CONCERN REGARDING LANTERN RAYNER." *YOU* DIDN'T SAY ANYTHING. I THOUGHT I WAS COMING HERE TO GET YOUR *ASHES* OR WHAT- EVER COSMIC DETRITUS WAS *LEFT* OF YOU!

UH... SORRY?

SORRY? *JUST* SORRY? THIS ISN'T PUTTING ME IN A NON-SLAPPY FRAME OF MIND, KYLE.

CAROL, I NEED YOU TO--

I'M REALLY GLAD YOU'RE NOT DEAD OR COSMIC DETRITUS OR PART OF A WALL.

AS ARE WE ALL, SAPPHIRE FERRIS.

ALL IS BETTER THEN, PAALKO FRIEND?

I COULD NOT *BEGIN* TO SPECULATE.

WHY?

WHAT?

WHY AM I THE ONLY PERSON WHO KNOWS YOU'RE ALIVE? I AM THE ONLY PERSON, RIGHT? OR ARE ALL THE LANTERN CORPS TRYING TO GASLIGHT ME?

BECAUSE...WELL, WHO ELSE AM I GOING TO TELL? SAINT WALKER IS IN A COMA, GUY IS A RED LANTERN, AND I CAN'T TELL JOHN BECAUSE HE'LL TELL HAL.

AND WHY CAN'T YOU TELL HAL? YOU KNOW HE DOESN'T ACTUALLY WANT YOU DEAD...

THERE ARE...THINGS THAT I HAVEN'T FIGURED OUT YET, AND--

THIS IS GOOD, EXCELLENT! I WANT FOR THINGS TO BE WELL, UNKNOWN FRIEND.

THIS IS NIAS EN THRODEN, WHO IS...

I AM NIAS DEN THRODEN, CRETCHLING OF NIAS DEN THRODEN, CRETCHLING OF GARA TAL THRODEN, KEEPER OF JOURNEYS, FRIEND TO OUTSIDERS--AND I AM HAPPY TO BE MAKING NEW FRIENDS.

HURM. YES, ALL THAT.

THE EXPLANATIONS AREN'T OVER, I HOPE YOU KNOW THAT.

REALLY?

I'M KYLE. LANTERN OF WHITE, FRIEND TO ANGRY WOMEN.

PLEASE TO BE FRIENDS.

I'M CAROL.

PLEASE TO BE CAROL FRIEND. I AM NIAS FRIEND.

SO WHY ARE WE HERE?

YOU ARE HERE BECAUSE LANTERN RAYNER WISHED FOR YOU TO BE HIS CONTACT WITH THE UNIVERSE AT LARGE, AND B--

NO, WHY ARE WE HERE. THIS PLANET. IS IT ABOUT TO BE INVADED, OR TURNED INSIDE OUT, OR ATTACKED BY SPACE SHARKS, OR WHAT?

AHA, CAROL FRIEND, I AM KNOWING THE ANSWER TO THIS. COME!

YOU KNOW ABOUT THE SPACE SHARKS?

EVERYBODY DOES.

WE ARE HERE--

YOU ARE HERE BECAUSE THIS IS EXURAS, AND EXURAS?

EXURAS IS *THE GREATEST PLACE IN THE UNIVERSE!*

AH, YOU DO NOT *BELIEVE,* RAYNER. COME...

OKAAAAY.

OH, THAT'S JUST WONDERFUL.

SEE.

SPONTANEOUS ALIEN SUICIDE. THAT'S... NEW-ISH?

IT IS NOT TO WORRY. EXURAS *PROVIDES.*

I DON'T SUPPOSE YOU'D CARE TO EXPLAIN *HOW* EXURAS PROVIDES?

WHERE WE COME FROM, HURLING YOURSELF OFF HIGH THINGS IS GENERALLY NOT CONSIDERED GOOD MANNERS. DEFINITELY NOT WITHOUT WARNING.

OR A PARACHUTE.

APOLOGIES, KYLE FRIEND. I AM NOT WISHING TO BE RUDE. EXURAS IS COVERED BY... I AM NOT SURE HOW WELL THIS WILL BE TRANSLATED. *"INTELLIGENT STRUCTURE"?*

I UNDERSTAND.

YOU DO, ZALLA FRIEND? THIS IS GOOD!

WE CAN SEE THEM IN THE ATMOSPHERE AND THE BUILDINGS. YOU WOULD PERHAPS UNDERSTAND THEM AS... COMPUTERIZED MOLECULES, KYLE.

THERE IS MORE TO THEM, BUT THAT MAY AID IN CLARITY.

IT DOES NOT.

THEY ARE *CONTROLLABLE.* THEY AR IN EVERYTHING. EVEN THE AIR. THE MONITOR, AND *REACT.*

THEY MAINTAIN THE BUILDINGS, SCRUB THE ATMOSPHERE OF TOXINS, AND, CLEARLY, INTERCEP KINETIC IMPACTS.

COME, GUARDIAN FRIENDS, I WILL SHOW YOU.

SO, I GUESS THAT'S WHAT WE'RE DOING.

IF YOU'RE MEANING TO GO INCOGNITO, I DON'T THINK THAT'S ACTUALLY GOING TO HELP.

MAYBE IF I HAD SOME GLASSES? OR PERHAPS A FEDORA.

WHOA!

HELLO, ALIEN FRIEND!

THEY *ARE* FRIENDLY, I'LL GIVE THEM THAT.

ARE YOU OKAY?

OKAY?

BACK THERE, WHEN THE ALIEN--

NIAS.

--WHEN NIAS DID HIS SWAN DIVE ACT, YOU *HESITATED.*

YOU'RE AFRAID TO USE THE RING.

I'M NOT.

KYLE--

I'M NOT. SERIOUSLY. I'M NOT. BUT...

CAROL, WE NEARLY BROUGHT IT ALL DOWN. THE UNIVERSE. EVERY-THING. THAT WAS *US.* NOT THE BAD GUYS. NOT SOME COSMIC BOGEYMAN. *US.*

AND I'M NOT SURE WE WON'T DO IT AGAIN.

I KNOW. I THINK EVEN HAL KNOWS. BUT *YOU'RE* HERE. YOU CAN REFILL THE RESERVOIR, IF WORSE COMES TO WORST.

AND THAT'S THE PROBLEM.

I DON'T KNOW IF THAT'S *TRUE.* PAALKO AND THE GUARDIANS DON'T KNOW EITHER. I DON'T *KNOW* IF I CAN REFILL IT AGAIN.

SO WHAT ARE YOU GOING TO DO? *STOP?* GIVE THE RING UP?

NO. I MEAN, MAYBE THAT'D BE THE BEST THING, BUT THE REAL PROBLEM IS THAT THERE *IS* NO OTHER WHITE LANTERN. IF *I'M* THE FAIL-SAFE...

AND WORSE, I DON'T KNOW IF I REFILLED IT FULLY THIS TIME. WE DID OUR LITTLE TRICK *WITHOUT* PARALLAX, SO WHO KNOWS WHAT THAT MEANS. THE ONLY PERSON WHO MIGHT--RELIC--IS NOW A GARGOYLE ON THE SOURCE WALL.

AND THE OTHER ENTITIES ARE GONE--MAYBE FOR GOOD.

...YOU *HAVE* TO KEEP THE RING. RIGHT. SO WHAT DOES THAT MEAN?

I WISH I KNEW. THAT'S WHY I'M HERE. I DON'T KNOW. I DON'T KNOW IF THE *GUARDIANS* KNOW. BUT I THINK THEY'RE MY BEST SHOT AT FIGURING IT OUT.

AND EXURAS IS PART OF THAT? OR ARE WE STILL IN THE "BILLION YEARS IN A BOX, SEE THE SIGHTS" PART OF THE PLAN?

NO...

...WE ARE NOT.

ZALLA. SO YOU HEARD ALL THAT?

I DID.

AND?

YOU WILL HAVE TO FORGIVE ME, CAROL. AS YOU SAY, I HAVE SPENT THE LAST FEW BILLION YEARS IN A BOX, WITH ONLY MY BROTHERS AND SISTERS FOR COMPANY. MY SOCIAL SKILLS MAY BE A BIT "RUSTY."

WE DO NOT KNOW THE ANSWERS TO THE QUESTIONS YOU AND KYLE HAVE. BUT WE HAVE CONSENSUS THAT THE CORPS IS NOT THE SOLUTION. SO OUR "MISSION" IS TO FIND ANOTHER WAY. A BETTER WAY.

SO WHY ARE WE HERE? IT CAN'T JUST BE BECAUSE THIS PLACE IS PARADISE?

IN FACT, THAT IS EXACTLY WHY WE ARE HERE, KYLE.

EXURAS USED TO BE A BACKWATER. UNTIL A CENTURY AGO, ITS TECHNOLOGY DEVELOPMENT WERE ROUGHLY ON A PAR WITH EARTH--AS WAS THEIR LEVEL OF STRIFE AND SUFFERING. NOT THE WORST IN THE UNIVERSE, BUT NOT THE BEST.

AND THAT CHANGED.

IT DID. OUR BROTHER YEKOP LEARNED ABOUT IT FROM THE RECORDS OF SEVERAL OF THE SHIPS STUDYING THE ANOMALY, AS THEY ALSO FELT IT WAS WORTH NOTE.

IN A GENERATION, EXURAS CHANGED FROM A BACKWATER TO SOMETHING APPROACHING UTOPIA.

AND WHAT DOES THAT TELL YOU?

THAT THERE'S STILL HOPE THAT EARTH WILL GET IT RIGHT?

THAT SOMEONE IS CONTROLLING THEM. THIS DOESN'T JUST HAPPEN. EITHER YOU CONTROL THEIR MINDS, OR YOU KILL EVERYONE WHO DOESN'T FIT.

OKAY, THAT'S GRIM.

IT IS. BUT NOT, I THINK, INCORRECT. KYLE IS RIGHT TO BE SUSPICIOUS.

THE PREVIOUS GUARDIANS TRIED TO CREATE UTOPIA. A LASTING PEACE. AND THEY FAILED. WORSE THAN FAILED, THEY LET IT TWIST THEM. SO I AM WARY OF ANY HEAVEN.

CERTAINLY, THE "INTELLIGENT STRUCTURE" TECHNOLOGY WOULD ALLOW FOR PERFECT SURVEILLANCE, AND PERFECT CONTROL.

EXCEPT.

THEY AREN'T?

NO, NOT SO FAR AS I CAN DETECT. THAT MEANS THAT THIS UTOPIA MAY BE GENUINE--AND THAT BRINGS US TO YOU, KYLE.

IF THIS UTOPIA IS GENUINE, IF WHAT THEY HAVE CAN BE REPLICATED, THEN THERE WILL BE NO NEED FOR THE CORPS. NO NEED TO RISK OUR UNIVERSE AGAIN.

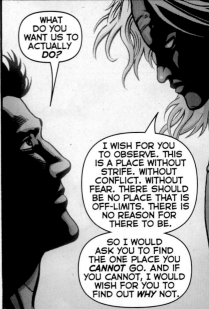

WHAT DO YOU WANT US TO ACTUALLY DO?

I WISH FOR YOU TO OBSERVE. THIS IS A PLACE WITHOUT STRIFE. WITHOUT CONFLICT. WITHOUT FEAR. THERE SHOULD BE NO PLACE THAT IS OFF-LIMITS. THERE IS NO REASON FOR THERE TO BE.

SO I WOULD ASK YOU TO FIND THE ONE PLACE YOU CANNOT GO. AND IF YOU CANNOT, I WOULD WISH FOR YOU TO FIND OUT WHY NOT.

WELL, I'M BEING BEJEWELED. *THAT'S* CLEARLY THE MARK OF A SINISTER MIND.

YOU KNOW THEY CAN HEAR YOU, RIGHT? YOU'RE TERRIBLE AT THIS WHOLE SPY THING.

HEAR, YES, UNDERSTAND, NOT SO MUCH. I HAD THE RING NOT TRANSLATE THAT. OR THIS.

...KYLE? LISTEN--

THINKING. YOU CAN FEEL LOVE?

MOSTLY, I FEEL ANNOYANCE. BUT I DON'T THINK THERE'S A COLOR FOR THAT. REDDISH?

I MEAN--

I KNOW WHAT YOU MEANT. I CAN DO THE THINKING THING TOO.

AND TO ANSWER THE QUESTION, YE I CAN DETECT LOV IN MY SURROUNDIN BUT SEEING AS IT PRETTY LITERALLY A AROUND US, I'M NO SURE HOW THAT' HELPING.

I CAN DETECT MORE THAN LOVE. WILL, HOPE AND COMPASSION WEREN'T HELPFUL.

BUT THERE *IS* FEAR HERE. SOME ANGER, TOO. BUT THE THING IS, IT'S ALL MOVING. IT'S ALL CONGREGATING...

...THERE.

"WELL, THAT MAKES SENSE. I GUESS IT'S TRUE EVERYWHERE IN THE UNIVERSE THAT IF YOU WANT FEAR AND ANGER..."

...TEENAGERS ARE THE WAY TO GO.

YEAH, THIS... I DON'T LIKE THIS, KYLE. ROUNDING UP THE YOUTH...I'VE SEEN THINGS LIKE THIS BEFORE. IN HISTORY BOOKS.

I KNOW. I SENT A SIGNAL FOR THE GUARDIANS TO COME AND TAKE A LOOK. BUT I DON'T INTEND TO WAIT...

WHATEVER THEY'RE DOING IN THERE, I WANT TO SEE IT.

PLEASE, STRANGER FRIEND, THIS IS NOT FOR YOU.

TRANGER IEND, LET SHOW YOU AT I HAVE MADE!

COME WITH ME--

NOT FOR YOU, STRANG--

FIND THE PLACE YOU CANNOT GO. WELL...

I'D SAY THIS QUALIFIES.

STOP.

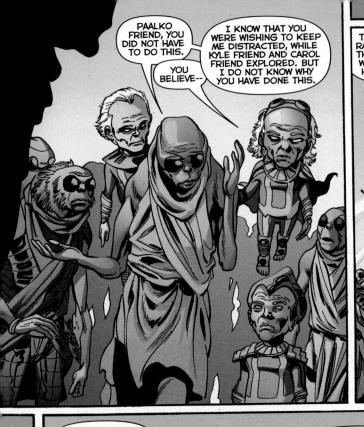

PAALKO FRIEND, YOU DID NOT HAVE TO DO THIS.

YOU BELIEVE--

I KNOW THAT YOU WERE WISHING TO KEEP ME DISTRACTED, WHILE KYLE FRIEND AND CAROL FRIEND EXPLORED. BUT I DO NOT KNOW WHY YOU HAVE DONE THIS.

THERE'S NO FEAR OR RAGE HERE, EXCEPT IN THE TEENAGERS. ZALLA WAS RIGHT, THEY *ARE* HIDING SOMETHING.

IT IS ALWAYS SO, WITH STRANGER FRIENDS. NONE UNDERSTAND.

THEN *HELP* US UNDERSTAND. SHOW US, NIAS DEN THRODEN, WHAT IT IS THAT YOU ARE HIDING.

HIDING? NO, THIS IS THE *OPPOSIT* OF HIDING. WHAT WE HA HERE, ALL OUR PEACE PROSPERITY, IT MAY ON EXIST SO LONG AS ALL EXURANS *SEE.*

THIS IS *NOT* A PLACE TO HIDE...

...THIS IS A PLACE TO SEE.

WOULD YOU SEE?

YES.

YES? *YES?* THIS HAS *REEDUCATION* CAMP WRITTEN ALL OVER IT.

I'M ABOUT 90% SURE IT DOES. BUT I'M 100% SURE THAT IF THERE'S SOME KIND OF MIND MOJO OR DISINTEGRATION CHAMBER IN THERE--

--THEN I'M THE ONE BEST EQUIPPED TO DEAL WITH IT, WHAT WITH EVERYONE AND THEIR BROTHER DECIDING TO HAVE FUN WITH KYLE'S BRAINMEATS LATELY.

KYLE--

YOU WANTED THIS, PAALKO.

SO I'M GOING.

WELCOME, FRIEND.

OKAY...

...THAT WAS SLIGHTLY ANTICLIMACTIC.

YOU, ON THE RAMP-- STOP.

WHAT RIGHT HAVE *YOU* TO TELL US TO STOP?

NONE. BUT I'M DOING IT ANYWAY. THIS DOESN'T FEEL RIGHT. AND IF YOU'RE HURTING THEM...

I AM.

NOT THE ANSWER YOU EXPECTED, THEN?

NOT EXACTLY, NO. MOST VILLAINS DON'T COME OUT AND SAY IT.

I AM TO BE THE *VILLAIN* IN THIS, THEN, FRIEND?

YOU'VE GOT THIS PRETTY, PERFECT PARADISE PLANET, AND YOU'VE GOT...WHATEVER THAT *BROKEN-MIRROR* THING IS, AND YOU'RE FEEDING *KIDS* INTO IT. YEAH, IT'S GOT THAT VILLAINOUS FEEL TO IT.

WOULD YOU LIKE TO *KNOW* WHAT THIS IS?

SURE.

OUR "PRETTY, PERFECT PARADISE PLANET" HAS A *COST*. THIS IS TRUE. AND OUR YOUNG ARE REQUIRED TO *DECIDE* WHETHER THIS PRICE IS WORTH PAYING. THIS, ALSO, IS TRUE. AND FOR SOME, THE PRICE IS PAINFUL.

DO YOU EVER WONDER WHAT THE WORLD WOULD BE LIKE IF JUST ONE SMALL THING HAD TURNED OUT DIFFERENTLY?

IMAGINE IF THE CREATURE THAT FLAPPED ITS TENTACLES AND CREATED THE STORM THAT LEFT THOUSANDS HOMELESS... HADN'T.

OR IF, INSTEAD OF BEING KILLED IN AN ACCIDENT, A YOUNG SCIENTIST MADE A DISCOVERY THAT COULD CHANGE THE LIVES OF *MILLIONS*.

NOW IMAGINE A WORLD WHERE EVERYTHING WENT JUST *EXACTLY* RIGHT. THE DESPOT ON THE VERGE OF WAR CHOKED ON HIS CLAGGASH. THE ARTIST WHO WOULD INSPIRE A GENERATION DIDN'T DIE AT BIRTH. IMAGINE A WORLD WHERE IT *ALL* WENT RIGHT.

WHAT DO YOU IMAGINE THAT WORLD WOULD BE LIKE?

PARADISE.

JUST SO. AND THIS IS WHAT ALLOWS US TO HAVE ALL THOSE PERFECT MOMENTS. BUT THERE IS A PRICE. YOU MUST SEE.

I'M GOING TO BE PISSED IF THIS ENDS UP BEING SOME SORT OF PORTAL TO...

...HELL.

THIS IS NOT HELL. THIS IS THE PRICE.

THE DEVICE ALLOWS US TO *CHANGE* THOSE MOMENTS. WHERE SOMETHING WENT WRONG IN OUR TIMELINE, IT WENT *RIGHT* SOMEWHERE ELSE.

WE *SWAP* THOSE MOMENTS.

YOU'RE STEALING THEIR FUTURE. TO CREATE A WORLD WHERE EVERYTHING HAS GONE RIGHT, YOU CREATED ONE WHERE EVERYTHING HAS GONE WRONG.

I DON'T UNDERSTAND.

NONE DO, AT FIRST. OUR WORLD IS ONE WHERE THE *BEST* OUTCOME IS THE ONE THAT *ALWAYS* OCCURS. THIS IS NOT CHANCE.

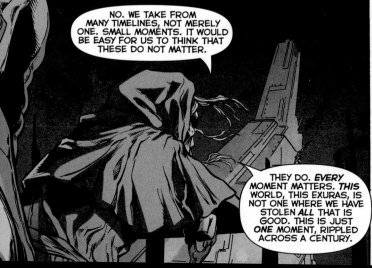

NO. WE TAKE FROM MANY TIMELINES, NOT MERELY ONE. SMALL MOMENTS. IT WOULD BE EASY FOR US TO THINK THAT THESE DO NOT MATTER.

THEY DO. *EVERY* MOMENT MATTERS. *THIS* WORLD, THIS EXURAS, IS NOT ONE WHERE WE HAVE STOLEN *ALL* THAT IS GOOD. THIS IS JUST *ONE* MOMENT, RIPPLED ACROSS A CENTURY.

THE PRICE.

AND YOUR PEOPLE. THEY JUST *ACCEPT* THAT? *ALL* OF THEM? KNOWING THAT THEIR PROSPERITY IS BUILT ON OTHER PEOPLE'S SUFFERING?

NOT ALL. THAT IS THE PURPOSE OF THIS JOURNEY.

"WE MUST DO THIS WITH OPEN EYES, FRIEND. ALL COME THROUGH THE GATES SO THAT THEY MAY SEE THE SACRIFICE THAT HAS BEEN MADE TO ALLOW THEM THEIR JOYOUS LIVES.

"AND SOME CANNOT BEAR IT. THEY CANNOT ACCEPT A WORLD BUILT ON THIS. THEY WILL NOT PAY THE PRICE.

"I SAID THIS HURTS THEM. AND IT DOES. IT SHOULD. THIS SHOULD NEVER BE EASY.

"THOSE THAT CANNOT ACCEPT OUR WORLD *STAY*, TRY TO MAKE THE MANY OTHER EXURAS BETTER PLACES. I CAN ONLY HOPE THAT THEY SUCCEED."

AND YOU THINK THAT MAKES IT *OKAY?!*

I DO. IF WE LEFT THOSE MOMENTS IN PLACE, MANY OF THE TIMELINES WOULD BE BETTER. BUT ONLY INCREMENTALLY. THERE ARE ONLY ENOUGH PERFECT MOMENTS TO CREATE *ONE* PERFECT PLACE.

AND ISN'T *ONE* PARADISE BETTER THAN AN *INFINITY* OF HELLS LESSENED?

NO. IT *ISN'T* WORTH IT. YOU DON'T HAVE THE RIGHT.

NO. BUT WE HAVE THE ABILITY. DO YOU HAVE A BETTER BASIS FOR WHATEVER IT IS THAT YOU MIGHT DO NEXT?

I--

SON OF--

SKLTCH

WAIT-- SOMEONE IS--

BOOM

NEED... NEED TO...

--GET BACK THROUGH THE DAMN *GATE.*

I KNOW--

COMING *THROUGH?* YES.

I AM NIAS DEN THRODEN, CRETCHLING OF NIAS DEN THRODEN CRETCHLING OF GAR TAL THRODEN.

WE HAVE BEEN A LONG TIME COMING "FRIEND."

WE WANT OUR FUTUR BACK.

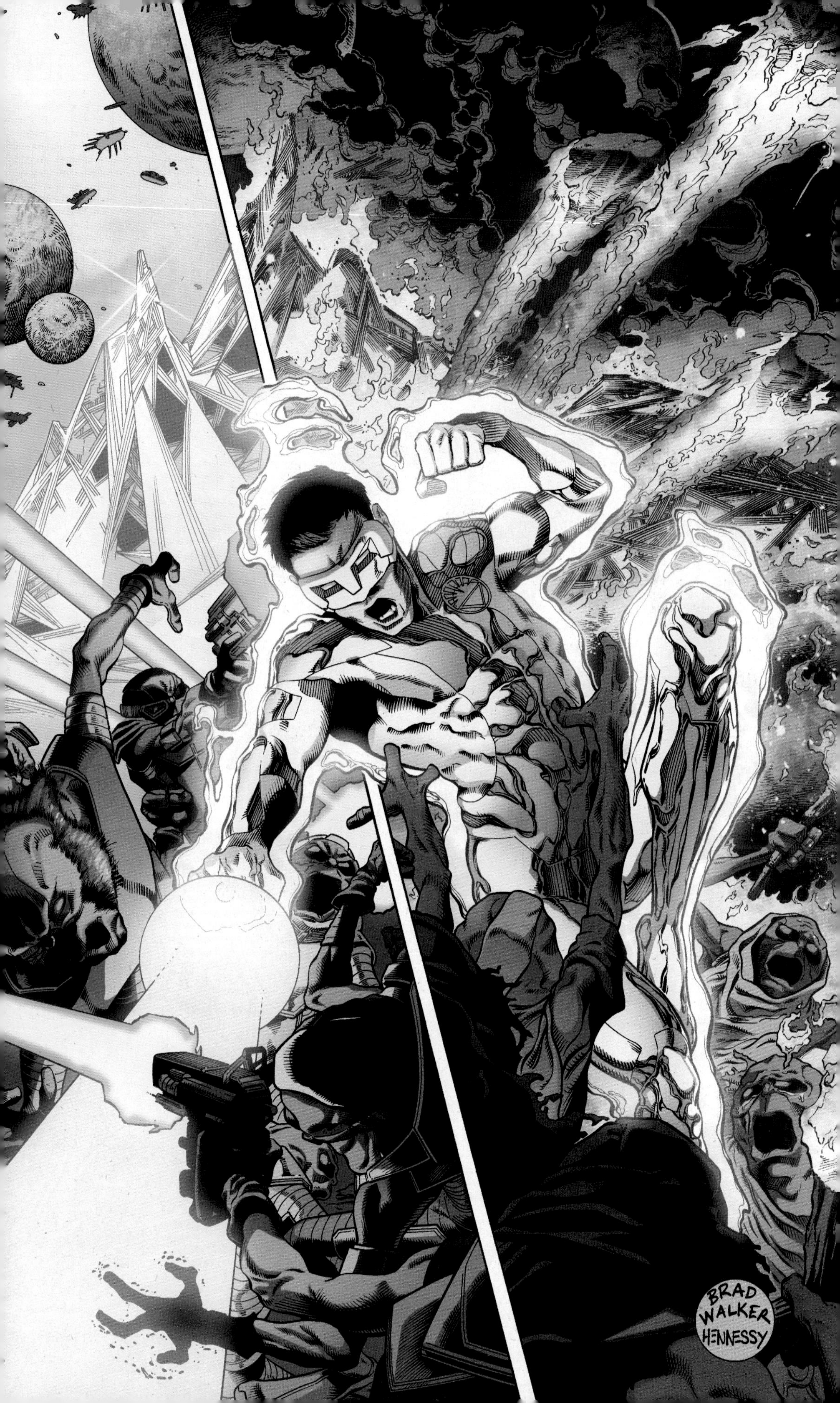
BRAD WALKER HENNESSY

YESTERDAY'S GONE
JUSTIN JORDAN writer BRAD WALKER & GERALDO BORGES pencillers
ANDREW HENNESSY, MARIAH BENES & J.P. MAYER inkers cover art by BRAD WALKER, ANDREW HENNESSY & WIL QUINTANA

YOU CAN STOP *RIGHT* THERE.

STEP BACK THROUGH THE PORTAL AND INTO YOUR TIMELINE.

KLK

I DO NOT THINK SO.

HAVE IT YOUR WAY. I TRIED.

THIS IS *PARADISE*, YES?

NO HITTING IN PARADISE, *FRIEND*.

THE *TECHNOLOGY* THEY *STOLE*--THEIR OMNIPRESENT "INTELLIGENT STRUCTURE"--WOULD NEVER ALLOW IT.

I'M WILLING TO TEST THAT THEORY. SO YOU'RE ANOTHER TIMELINE'S *VERSION* OF *NIAS*, THEN? I LIKE THE O.G. ONE BETTER.

HE HASN'T THROWN A *SPEAR* THROUGH ANYONE RIGHT IN FRONT OF ME.

LET'S SEE HOW THE "STRUCTURE" LIKES A *FULL POWER*--

NO!

THE INTELLIGENT STRUCTURE IS AN INTEGRATED SYSTEM. IN ORDER TO COMPENSATE FOR THE KINETIC ENERGY YOU'RE EXPENDING, IT HAS TO DRAW MASS AND ENERGY FROM NON-LOCAL SOURCES AND--

AND WHAT YEKOP IS *TRYING* TO SAY, LANTERN RAYNER, IS THAT IF YOU KEEP PUSHING, THE ENTIRE *CITY* WILL TEAR ITSELF APART TRYING TO *STOP* YOU.

OKAY, ZALLA. BUT I'M PRETTY SURE THAT DOESN'T MEAN I CAN'T *STOP* THEM WITH A CONSTRUCT.

THEY ARE GOING TO STAY RIGHT WHERE THEY ARE.

I'M GOING TO FIX THIS, GRANDFATHER. THE BLUE LIGHT CAN HEAL YOU.

I JUST NEED TO REPAIR ENOUG DAMAGE TO TAKE THIS SPEAR OUT. *HOLD ON...*

NOW *THIS* IS INTERESTING. ANOTHER STOLEN MIRACLE, MAYBE?

AH, NO. I THINK YOU WILL NOT BE DOING THAT. THE INTELLIGENT STRUCTURE WILL NOT LET ME HIT, THIS IS TRUE...

"BUT I CAN STILL *KILL*, I THINK."

BOOOOM

NO!

KLK

SOMETHING ISN'T RIGHT. THE HARD CODE OF THE STRUCTURE SYSTEM IS *CHANGING*. I DON'T THINK THAT SHOULD BE.

CAROL, I NEED YOU TO GET ALL THE OTHER EXURANS OUT OF HERE...

BECAUSE THERE IS *DEFINITELY* GOING TO BE A FIGHT.

GUARDIANS, GET READY--

GOT IT.

OH, I SEE. HE'S SUBVERTED THE COMMAND SYSTEM. I WONDER IF HE CAN....

FIGHT?

KRRKKKOOOOOOOOOOM

I WOULD NOT CALL IT A *FIGHT*, FRIEND.

GET BEHIND ME!

HE'S TAKEN *CONTROL* OF THE STRUCTURE! EVERYTHING IN EXURAS--

KYLE!

UNGH!

NIAS, THIS IS...

NECESSARY. CAN YOU DO WHAT IS NEEDED?

THE TECHNOLOGY IS MINE. *THEIR* GRANDFATHER... THE...*OTHER* ME... HIS EQUATIONS WERE RIGHT.

IS THAT AN ANSWER?

YES. IT WILL NOT TAKE LONG.

I'VE *GOT* YOUR SOLDIERS, YOU MONSTER. AND YOU ARE GOING BACK THROUGH THAT GATE.

THIS STRUCTURE IS *USEFUL*, PROPERLY DIRECTED. *VERY* USEFUL.

ALL OF YOU. IF I CAN'T BLAST YOU OR HIT YOU I WILL *DRAG* YOU THROUGH MYSELF--

WILL YOU?

THE STRUCTURE IS RECONFIGURED FOR MASS PORTAL TRANSITION, BUT *OTHER* FUNCTIONS MAY BE COMPROMISED...

WHERE WOULD YOU TAKE US...

TAP TIK TAP

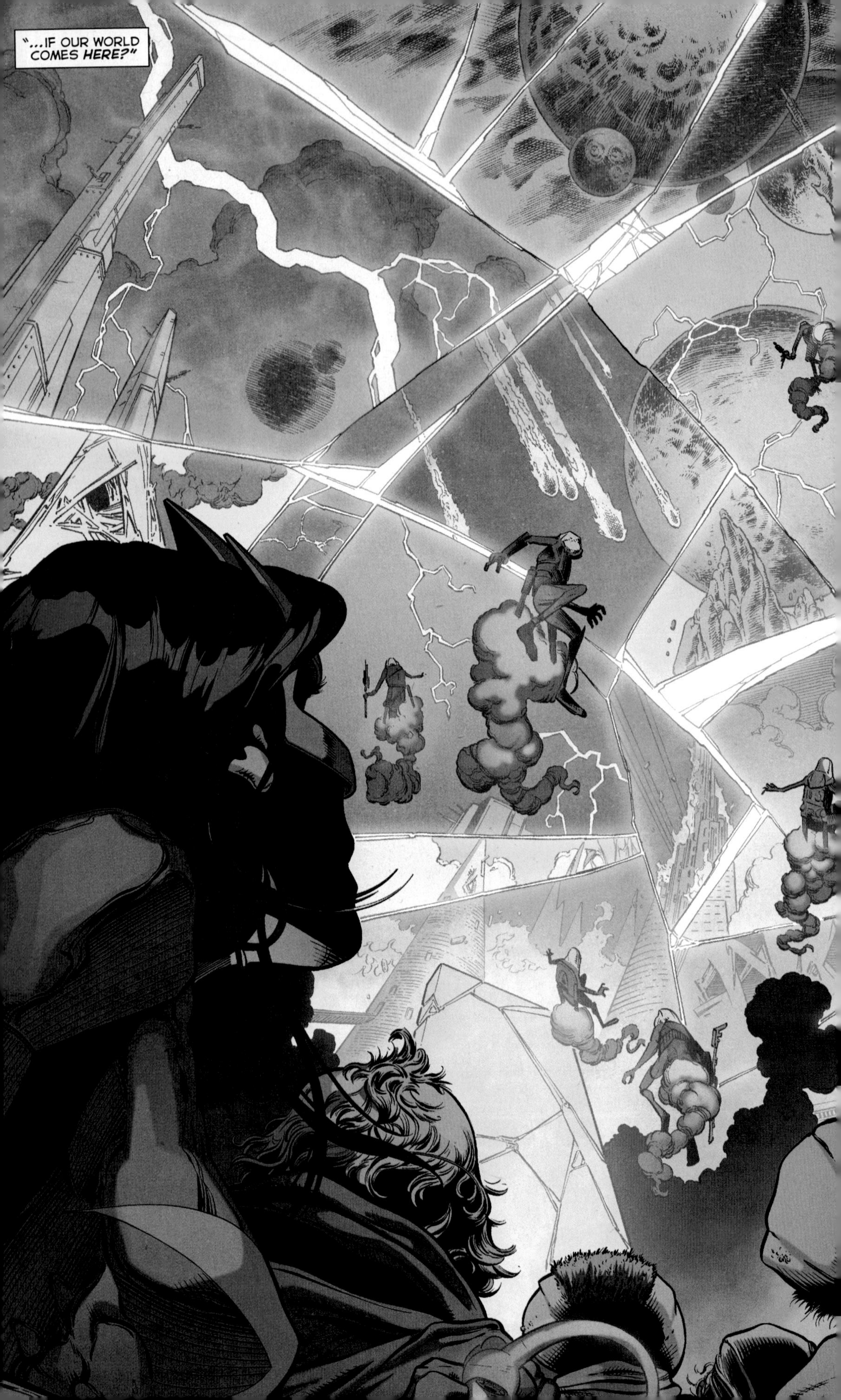
"...IF OUR WORLD COMES HERE?"

THAT IS SO VERY, VERY NOT GOOD.

SO MANY TIMELINES... IT'S NOT POSSIBLE--

YOU HAVE NOT EVEN BEGUN TO SEE WHAT IS POSSIBLE, THIEF.

YOU THOUGHT THAT SIMPLY LETTING YOUR CHILDREN SEE WHAT YOU DID TO US WAS ENOUGH?

THEN SEE WHAT WE DO.

YEAH, NO.

OR PERHAPS YOU WILL NOT *LIVE* TO SEE.

AH! THANK YOU, FRIEND. THE STRUCTURE...

HAS BEEN RECONFIGURED INTO A MINIATURE FOURTH-DIMENSION FOR MECHANISM. AMAZING AMAZING! BUT IT CAN'T THAT *AND* MAINTAIN TH KINETIC-DISSOLUTION FUNCTION, APPARENTLY.

WHICH MEANS THAT KYLE--

I'VE GOT SOME OPTIONS.

DO ANY OF THOSE OPTIONS INVOLVE HELPING ME?

BECAUSE I DON'T THINK I CAN FIGHT THIS GUY'S ARMY AND PROTECT THE XURANS AT THE SAME TIME...

THIS ISN'T AS EASY AS IT LOOKS.

JUST DO WHAT YOU CAN!

THE STRUCTURE, IT IS NOT DESIGNED FOR THIS. IT IS TOO MUCH. TOO *MUCH!*

THE STRUCTURE IS--

YES, YEKOP, WE UNDERSTAND THE SITUATION.

AND WE DO NOT INTEND TO ALLOW THIS TO CONTINUE.

WAIT, WHERE ARE YOU GOING?

KYLE HAS CREATED AN OPPORTUNITY FOR US TO BRING THIS TO A CONCLUSION.

AND IN THE MEANTIME, WE SHOULD...?

I FEEL STOPPING THE CITY FROM FALLING WOULD BE AN EXCELLENT START, CAROL.

THIS ISN'T RIGHT. WHAT THEY DID TO YOU...I DON'T EVEN HAVE THE WORDS TO EXPLAIN IT.

BUT YOU CAN'T *DESTROY* THEIR WORLD. *THIS* ISN'T THE ANSWER.

THEY STOLE THEIR PARADISE FROM *US*. YOU DO NOT SEE. YOU DO NOT *KNOW*.

WHAT I HAVE LOST BECAUSE OF THEM...WHAT THEY STOLE FROM ME. FROM US. THEY HAVE STOLEN OUR HAPPY ENDINGS.

I WILL HAVE THEM *BACK*--

OR I WILL TEAR THEIR PARADISE DOWN.

YOU SHALL NOT PASS--

I RATHER THINK WE SHALL.

ZALLA, WE ARE SO MUCH MORE POWERFUL THAN THEY ARE...DO YOU THINK IT RIGHT TO--

BROTHER, I WISH THAT WE HAD TIME FOR A REASONED DEBATE WITH THEM OVER THE MERITS OF OUR CAUSE. BUT WE DO NOT. THEY WILL RECOVER.

YOU...AH....YOU SHOULD NOT ATTACK HIM. I DO NOT BELIEVE RENDERING THEIR GRANDFATHER UNCONSCIOUS WILL RETURN THE GATE TO ITS ORIGINAL STATE, AND I...AH...DON'T KNOW HOW.

SORRY?

IT'S FINE, YEKOP. THIS IS NOT OUR FIGHT.

IT IS NIAS'.

I AM TO BE SORRY, GRAND-FATHER...

I'M TRYING TO BE REASONABLE. I'M *TRYING* TO HELP. YOU ARE NOT MAKING THIS EASY OR, FOR THAT MATTER, A VERY APPEALING OPTION.

WHY *DO* YOU HELP THEM? THEY ARE THIEVES. PLUNDERERS ON A SCALE THAT CAN SCARCELY BE IMAGINED.

BECAUSE WHAT YOU'RE DOING WILL BE *WORSE.* WOULD YOU KILL THEM ALL, IF YOU COULD?

I WOULD KILL THEM A *BILLION* TIMES OVER FOR ONE MORE MOMENT WITH MY WIFE. MY CHILDREN. BUT THAT FUTURE WAS STOLEN FROM ME.

THIS IS...NOT AS PLANNED. I DID NOT EXPECT THEM TO BE...

PEOPLE.

I HAD IMAGINED THEM MONSTERS.

AND I HAVE HAD *ENOUGH* OF CAGES. AT LEAST THIS ONE I CAN SEE.

DO YOU KNOW, "FRIEND," WHAT IT IS LIKE TO BE TRAPPED IN A CAGE YOU NEVER EVEN KNEW WAS THERE?

I DO. IT JUST IS AN EXCU

I THOUGHT YOU CALLOUS. *COLD.* BUT...

WE ARE NOT. I AM BEGGING OF YOU, PLEASE STOP THIS. LOOK AT WHAT HE IS DOING. WHAT YOU ARE *BOTH* DOING.

YOU STOLE SO MUCH FROM US.

EXCUSE? I DON'T NEED AN EXCUSE, ANY MORE THAN THEY DID. I HAVE A REASON. THAT IS *ENOUGH.*

BUT THIS VIOLENCE WILL NOT GIVE IT BACK. THIS IS NOT JUSTICE. THIS IS ONLY VENGEANCE.

KEEP PUSHING, AND YOU WILL RUPTURE THE STRUCTURE. I DO NOT KNOW WHAT WILL HAPPEN IF YOU DO, ALTHOUGH CERTAINLY MANY OF THEM WILL DIE. *STOP.*

YOU-- FIRST--

I SUSPECTED AS MUCH. LET US SEE HOW DURABLE YOU ARE.

ALL WE WANTED WAS TO *LIVE* IN THIS PARADISE...

I THOUGHT WE WERE COMING TO TAKE OUR MIRACLES *BACK.* I DID NOT WANT TO *BUTCHER* YOU ALL...

IT WAS NOT SUPPOSED TO *BE* LIKE THIS!

THEN DO NOT *LET* IT BE LIKE THIS.

THIS IS OVER.

YOU'RE RIGHT ABOUT THAT...

LOOK AROUND YOU.

FINALLY.

NO...THE PORTALS... WHAT HAVE YOU DONE?

I JUST NEEDED TO KEEP YOU DISTRACTED LONG ENOUGH FOR THE GUARDIANS TO SHUT DOWN THE GATE AND FOR YOU TO GET CLOSE ENOUGH...

...TO DO THIS.

NO--

NOT NOW, NOT *NOW*--

NO!

THE DOOHICKEY YOU USED TO CONTROL THE *INTELLIGENT STRUCTURE* WASN'T MADE OF THE SAME STUFF. IT WAS VULNERABLE.

I JUST NEEDED TO MAKE SURE THE GATES WERE *CLOSED* BEFORE I COULD TEST THE THEORY.

THEY CANNOT BE ALLOWED TO DO THIS! I WILL *DIE* BEFORE I STOP!

I KNOW.

AND I PROBABLY *CAN'T* STOP YOU FROM THE "DIE" PART. BUT I WANT YOU TO *SEE* THIS.

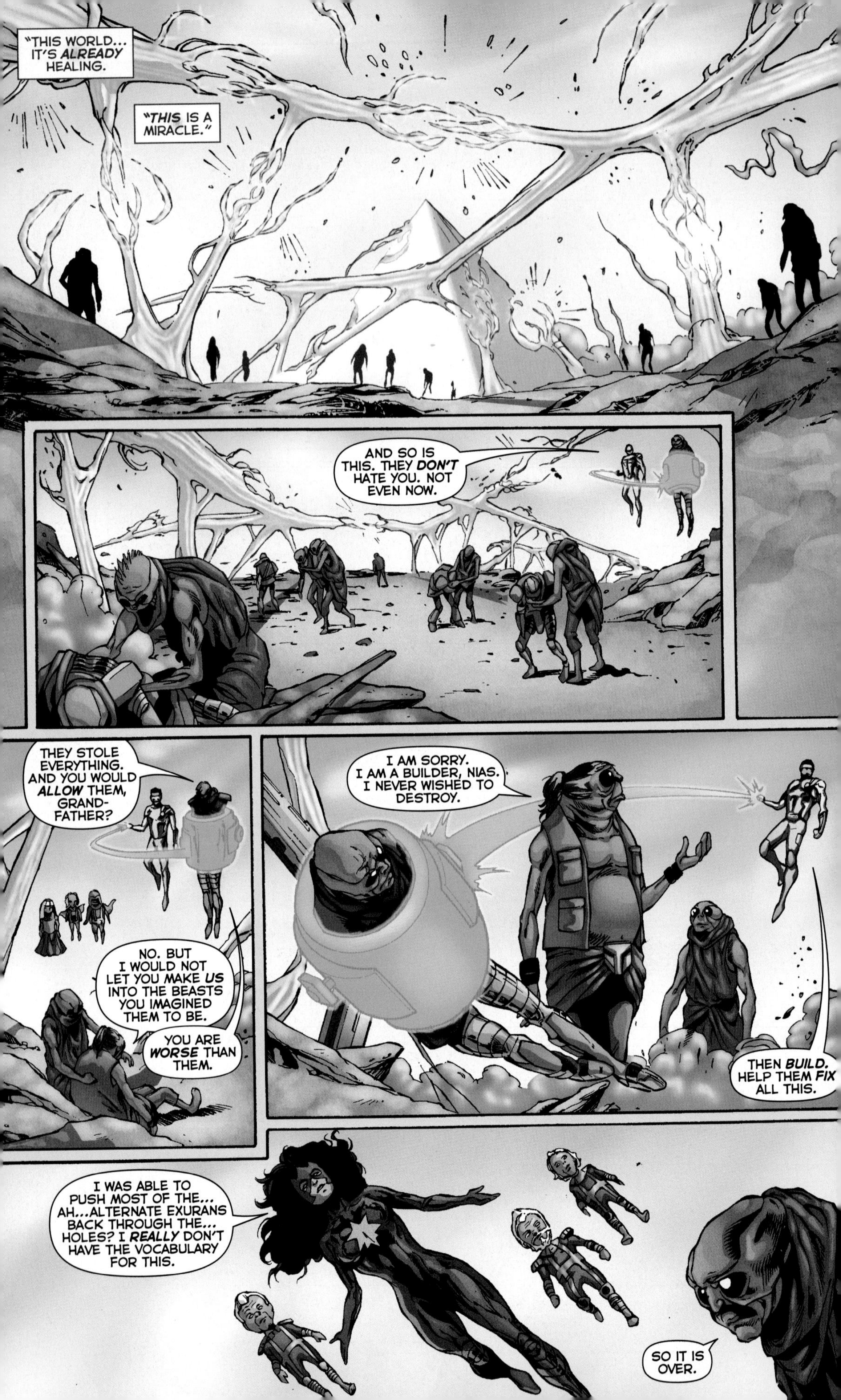
"THIS WORLD... IT'S *ALREADY* HEALING.
"*THIS* IS A MIRACLE."
AND SO IS THIS. THEY *DON'T* HATE YOU. NOT EVEN NOW.
THEY STOLE EVERYTHING. AND YOU WOULD *ALLOW* THEM, GRAND-FATHER?
NO. BUT I WOULD NOT LET YOU MAKE *US* INTO THE BEASTS YOU IMAGINED THEM TO BE.
YOU ARE *WORSE* THAN THEM.
I AM SORRY. I AM A BUILDER, NIAS. I NEVER WISHED TO DESTROY.
THEN *BUILD.* HELP THEM *FIX* ALL THIS.
I WAS ABLE TO PUSH MOST OF THE... AH...ALTERNATE EXURANS BACK THROUGH THE... HOLES? I *REALLY* DON'T HAVE THE VOCABULARY FOR THIS.
SO IT IS OVER.

YOU'RE NOT OFF THE HOOK, NIAS.

YOU'RE AS BAD AS...OTHER-YOU, I GUESS. YOU *SEE*, BUT YOU DON'T *FEEL*. THE OTHER NIAS LET HIS RAGE CONSUME HIM UNTIL ALL HE CARED ABOUT WAS HURTING YOU AS MUCH AS YOU HURT HIM.

BUT YOU *DID* HURT THEM.

AND YOU *NEED* TO FEEL IT. YOU HURT THESE PEOPLE SO BADLY I'M NOT SURE THERE'S ANY MAKING IT RIGHT. BUT YOU *ARE* GOING TO TRY.

BUT WE COULD NOT...THERE WAS NOT *ENOUGH* FOR ALL. WAS IT NOT BETTER TO HAVE ONE PARADISE THAN NONE?

I DON'T KNOW. I REALLY DON'T. BUT YOU COULD HAVE USED THE GATE TO SEED THE TECHNOLOGY YOU HAVE THROUGHOUT THE TIMELINES. YOU COULD HAVE MADE IT *ALL* BETTER, FOR EVERYONE.

BUT YOU DIDN'T. INSTEAD YOU *WATCHED*, AND TOLD YOURSELF THAT WHAT LITTLE HELP YOU GAVE THEM--FROM PEOPLE TOO *GUILTY* TO LIVE IN PARADISE WHILE OTHERS SUFFERED-- WAS ENOUGH.

IT *WASN'T*. AND IT ENDS NOW.

MAKE THIS *RIGHT*. OR I WILL.

HOW DO WE MAKE THIS RIGHT, FRIENDS?

DO AS KYLE SAYS. ALL THE TIMELINES YOU'VE STOLEN FROM, SHARE. GIVE THEM THE CHANCE TO BE BETTER.

AND WHEN YOU'VE DONE SO, DESTROY THE GATE TECHNOLOGY. THAT IS FAR TOO DANGEROUS FOR ANY WORLD TO HAVE. AND IF YOU DO NOT...

WE WILL ALL RETURN. AND YOU WILL NOT LIKE IT.

SO... WE'RE DONE HERE?

I AM. BUT I DON'T TELL YOU WHAT TO DO.

JUST THE EXURANS, THEN.

DO YOU HAVE A PROBLEM WITH WHAT I DID?

DO YOU? BECAUSE, FRANKLY, LAYING DOWN EDICTS DOESN'T FEEL LIKE YOU, KYLE.

MAYBE NOT. BUT I...

I'VE GOT ALL THIS POWER, BUT EVEN SO, SOMETIMES THE BEST SOLUTION IS A BAD ONE. I COULDN'T LET THEM KEEP STEALING FUTURES. SO IF I HAVE TO BE THE ONE TO LAY DOWN THE LAW...

...SO BE IT.

AND DID YOU LEARN WHAT YOU WISHED TO LEARN FROM ALL THIS, THEN?

NO. LANTERN RAYNER DOES NOT UNDERSTAND WHAT HE SAW BEYOND THE SOURCE WALL. BUT THEY ARE COMING...

AND HE IS NOT READY.

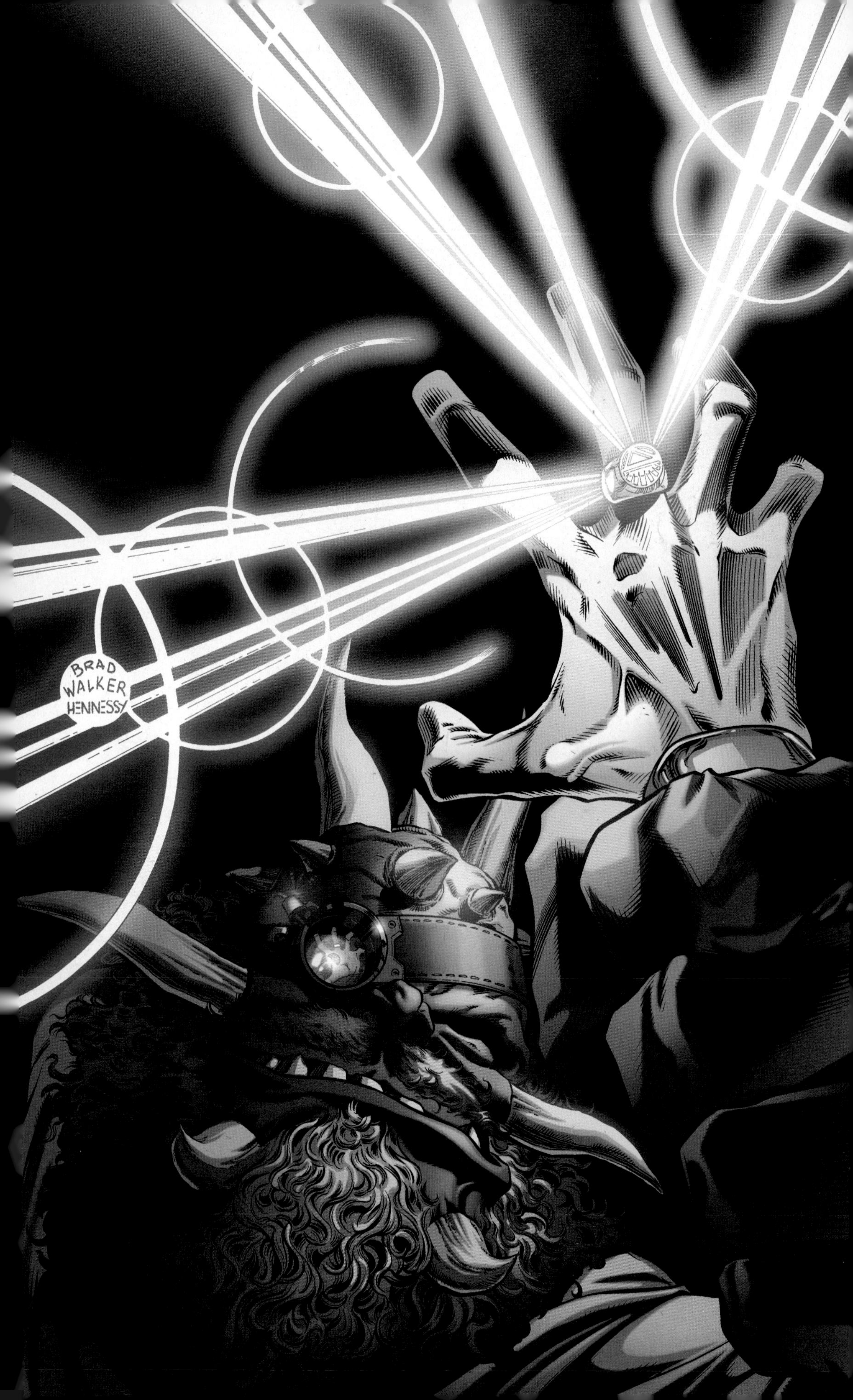
BRAD WALKER HENNESSY

KEEPER

JUSTIN JORDAN writer **ANDREI BRESSAN** artist
cover art by **BRAD WALKER, ANDREW HENNESSY & WIL QUINTANA**

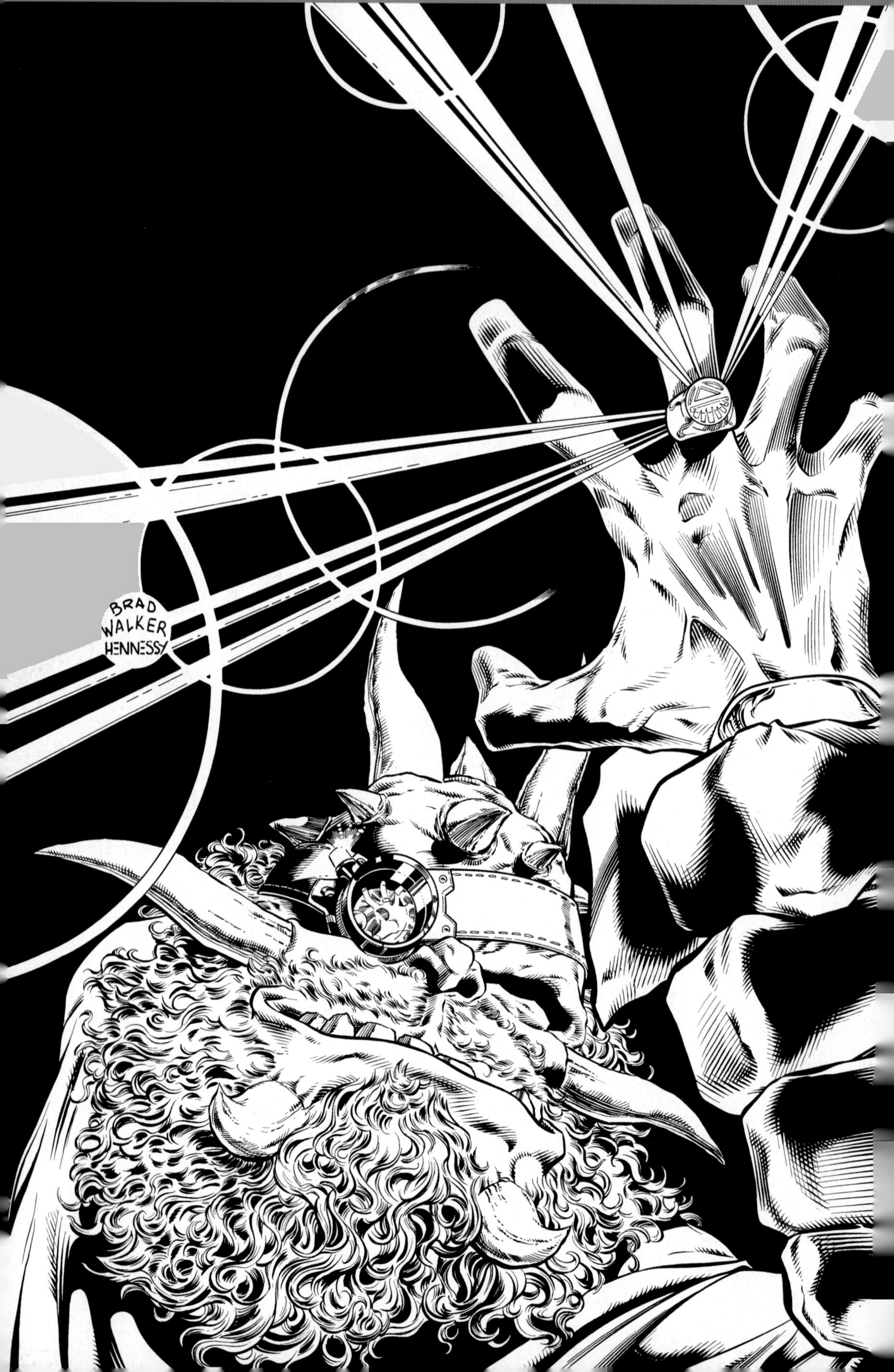
BRAD WALKER HENNESSY

THIS IS WRONG.

THESE ARE MY PEOPLE--THE KALIMAWANS...

BUT THEY ARE NOT THE PEOPLE I REMEMBER.

BEFORE I LEFT TO GUARD THE ANOMALY AT THE EDGE OF THE UNIVERSE, WE WERE AT PEACE.

THIS IS NO LONGER THE CASE.

YOU WILL ANSWER FOR WHAT YOU HAVE DONE, PARASITE.

I DO NOT KNOW WHAT HAS HAPPENED IN MY ABSENCE, BUT I KNOW THAT THIS--?

--THIS IS UNACCEPTABLE.

NO.

STOP THIS FOOLISH-NESS.

THIS IS NOT AN ISOLATED INCIDENT.

AS I HAVE MADE MY WAY HOME FROM THE RUINS OF THE ANOMALY, I HAVE FOUND MY PEOPLE INCITING CONFLICT WITH EVERYONE IN MY PATH.

EXETER. THE KEEPER.

YOU WOULD PROTECT THE MUSCARIANS? OUR HATED ENEMY?

THEY ARE INNOCENT.

"KEEPER." NO. YOU DO NOT DESERVE THAT TITLE. NOT AFTER YOU BETRAY US LIKE THIS.

I AM EXETER. I DO NOT BETRAY.

AND I DO NOT FAIL.

...YOU SHOULD NOT HAVE COME HERE ALONE.

WHAT MAKES YOU THINK I WOULD BE SO UNWISE...

I KNOW WHAT YOU ARE. AND I KNOW THAT...

...AS TO COME HERE ALONE?

YOU KNOW, I DON'T *NORMALLY* LIKE HITTING PEOPLE IN THE BACK, BUT I *CAN* MAKE AN EXCEPTION.

YOU ARE LATE, KYLE RAYNER.

YOU TRY FINDING ONE TINY SHIP IN ALL OF KNOWN SPACE, EXETER. YOU'RE LUCKY WE'RE HERE AT ALL.

FWUMP

DO YOU NEED A HAND?

...BUT UNNECESSARY. THE MATTER IS IN HAND.

OR FOOT, POSSIBLY.

YOUR OFFER IS APPRECIATED...

I DID NOT ASK YOU TO COME HERE TO HELP ME DEFEAT THESE CHILDREN, CAROL FERRIS.

YOU DIDN'T?

NO, NO, GUYS, JUST STAY DOWN. GET COZY.

WE HAVE IMPORTANT BUSINESS ELSEWHERE, EXETER. WHAT IS IT THAT YOU REQUIRE OF US?

I NEED NO HELP ENDING SMALL BATTLES SUCH AS THESE, PAALKO. I MAY NEED YOU GUARDIANS TO HELP ME END A WAR.

YOUR PEOPLE ARE AT WAR WITH THE MUSCARIANS? THAT SEEMS... UNLIKELY.

IT IS IMPOSSIBLE, ZALLA. THE MUSCARIANS ARE INCAPABLE OF VIOLENCE.

I BUY THAT. I MEAN, JUST LOOK AT 'EM. ANY INSIGHT AS TO WHY YOUR FOLKS ARE ATTACKING THE FUNGI?

I DO NOT KNOW. I SPENT A GREAT DEAL OF TIME AWAY FROM HOME. MANY THINGS HAVE CHANGED. BUT THI CANNOT ONE OI THEM.

TRAITOR.

YES, YOU SAID. WHY HAVE YOU AMBUSHED THESE MUSCARIANS?

WHY? YOU WOULD ASK US WHY? THEY HAVE BEEN VICIOUSLY ATTACKING OUR COLONIES FOR HUNDREDS OF YEARS, AND THIS SHIP--

ENOUGH.

YOU KNOW, I COULD HAVE JUST GAGGED HIM.

I DO KNOW.

THE YOUNG ONE CLEARLY *BELIEVES* THEY ARE YOUR ENEMIES...

YOUR ACTIONS DESTROYED THE ANOMALY, AND *ENDED* MY ROLE FOR THE FIRST TIME IN HISTORY. BUT MY *RESPONSIBILITY* TO MY PEOPLE STILL STANDS.

I WOULD ASK YOU TO HELP. I FEEL I AM OWED.

WE'LL HELP IF WE CAN.

THE KEEPER IS THE PROTECTOR OF THE ANOMALY AT THE EDGE OF OUR TERRITORY. BUT HE IS ALSO THE PROTECTOR OF THE ENTIRE KALIMAWAN RACE.

FROM EXILE, HE WATCHES OVER ALL. HE IS HONORED.

WE CAN, LANTERN RAYNER.

WHICH IS WHY I REQUIRE YOUR HELP.

YOU MUST UNDERSTAND-- I AM THE KEEPER.

THIS IS REMARKABLE. YOUR PEOPLE HAVE *AUGMENTED* THEIR COGNITIVE ABILITIES WITH A BIOMETRIC NET, GIVING THEM ACCESS TO MNEMONIC CAP--

YOUR PEOPLE HAVE TAKEN UP THE USE OF AN *EXOCORTEX*, TO BOOST MEMORY STORAGE AND THEIR INTELLECTUAL CAPABILITIES.

BUT SOMEONE *HAS* EXPLOITED THEIR DEPENDENCE ON THIS TO ALTER THEIR MEMORIES. THEY WERE NOT ATTACKED BY THE MUSCARIANS--YET THEY *REMEMBER* IT.

SO THEY BUILT THEMSELVES EXTRA BRAINS.

AND THEN SOMEONE *HACKED* THEM.

WHY? TO MAKE THEM GO TO WAR? TO *WHAT END?*

I DO NOT KNOW. BUT CLEARLY, THE ANSWERS LIE *ELSEWHERE...*

THIS IS NOT HOW I WOULD PREFER TO RETURN TO MY HOME, AFTER DECADES ALONE AT MY POST... IN A STOLEN SHIP, SKULKING LIKE A COWARD.

THIS IS... COZY. IN A HARSH, MILITARY KIND OF WAY.

I'M NOT GOING TO LIE, I SORT OF MISS SITTING DOWN WHILE TRAVELING. FLOATING GETS A LITTLE OLD.

THOUGH OTHERS SEEM TO BE ENJOYING THIS.

...THIS IS NOT A KALIMAWAN SHIP.

IT IS NOT?

NO. WELL, I MEAN, YES, THE DESIGN SPECIFICATIONS WERE CLEARLY CREATED WITH KALIMAWAN PHYSIOLOGY IN MIND...

BUT I HAVE CROSS-REFERENCED THIS TECHNOLOGY WITH THAT WHICH YOU USE IN YOUR DEFENSIVE SHIELD AND--

FEWER WORDS, MORE MEANING.

HE COMPARED YOUR TECHNOLOGY TO THOSE OF THIS SHIP.

AND THIS IS NOT THE RESULT OF ADVANCES WHILE I WAS ABSENT?

OH NO. NO NO. DEFINITELY NOT. TECHNOLOGICAL PROGRESS DEVELOPS ALONG SPECIFIC PATHS. THE INHERENT LOGIC, THE MATHEMATICAL AESTHETICS, THEY ARE ALL--

YEKOP MEANS "NO."

"BECAUSE *THAT* CONCERNS ME."

SO YEAH, ALL THAT. DOES IT HAVE ANYTHING TO DO WITH *THAT?*

THIS IS...

A SHIPYARD. ON A MASSIVE SCALE. THEY ARE CONSTRUCTING A FLEET.

THIS IS MORE THAN A FLEET. THIS IS SUFFICIENT MILITARY POWER TO CONQUER *STAR SYSTEMS.*

THIS IS ALSO WHERE THE EXOCORTEX INFORMATION IS BEING REDIRECTED. I THINK. IF WE FOLLOW IT TO...

"...THE CORE."

I'M TAKING US IN. WELL, THE *SHIP* IS, ANYWAY--THEY HAVE THEIR DOCKING PROCESS AUTOMATED.

LET US TAKE THE LEAD. WE *SHOULD* HAVE THE ELEMENT OF SURPRISE, BUT IT....

...WON'T LAST LONG.

OR AT ALL.

WHY DOESN'T *ANYTHING* EVER GO ACCORDING TO PLAN?

YIELD!

I THINK IT'S YOU. I THINK YOU HAVE A NATURAL ANTI-PLAN QUALITY.

IT WAS A GOOD PLAN!

DOES THIS SEEM LIKE AN APPROPRIATE TIME FOR ROMANTIC BANTER?

HE MIGHT HAVE A POINT.

WAIT, ROMANTIC?

FOCUS. BECAUSE...

...HERE THEY COME.

TRAITOR! YOU WILL FALL!

I AM SORRY YOU FEEL THAT WAY.

BUT YOU ARE WRONG. IN ALL THINGS. I AM THE KEEPER. AND ONE WAY OR ANOTHER...

...YOU WILL YIELD.

THEY ARE CLEARLY TRYING TO KEEP US CONTAINED HERE... OR KILL US. I THINK THEY'RE PRETTY FOND OF THE "OR KILL US" OPTION.

DO YOU HAVE A SUGGESTION, PAALKO?

I DO, SAPPHIRE FERRIS, AND IT IS THE SAME FOR EITHER OPTION.

DO NOT *LET* THEM.

YOU HEARD THE MAN.

TERRIFIC. DO YOU HAVE A PARTICULAR DESTINATION IN MIND?

WELL, I'M NOT ANY KIND OF TACTICAL GENIUS OR ANYTHING, BUT I'M THINK-ING...

"...THE DOOR?"

YOU WILL OPEN.

ACTIONS SPEAK LOUDER.

I WOULD HAVE SUCCEEDED.

EVENTUALLY.

I KNOW. NOW LET'S JUST FIND WHO'S DOING THIS.

I'M NOT SURE YELLING AT INANIMATE OBJECTS IS ALL THAT HELPFUL, EXETER.

WELL, THEN...

...MISSION ACCOMPLISHED.

DO YOU REMEMBER THE LAST TIME YOU OPENED A DOOR AND SOMEONE *WASN'T* WAITING TO KILL US?

NOT EVEN A LITTLE.

YOU WILL UNDO THIS ATROCITY--

OR?

THWAM

I GOT HIM.

I GOT *HIM*.

NOW *THIS* IS INTERESTING.

I'M GLAD YOU'RE ENTERTAINED. NOW, WHO EXACTLY *ARE* YOU? BECAUSE I DON'T BELIEVE FOR EVEN A *SECOND* YOU'RE ONE OF EXETER'S PEOPLE.

NOT WITH *THAT* VOICE.

TRUTH. THIS BODY IS A SKIN I WEAR. BUT DESPITE MY POWER, I AM A HUMBLE TRADER. PROVIDING *ARMS* TO THOSE WHO NEED TO SOLVE THEIR CONFLICTS IN A...DECISIVE MANNER IS ONE SUCH TRADE.

PERCEPTIVE! THE KALIMAWANS, WITH THEIR ARTIFICIAL OUTBOARD MEMORIES, HAVE MADE IT SO EASY. NORMALLY, I WOULD HAVE TO SEND AN EXTENSION OF MYSELF TO A PLANET FOR *DECADES* TO ENGINEER PROFITABLE CONDITIONS.

I AM *QUITE* INTERESTED IN *YOURS.*

JUST A *WARMONGER,* THEN.

AND IF THERE IS NO CONFLICT TO BE FOUND, YOU *MANUFACTURE* ONE?

I AM CALLED A LOT OF THINGS, BUT "WARMONGER" DOES HAVE A CERTAIN RING TO IT. AND *SPEAKING* OF RINGS...

KYLE!

SHOULD HAVE...SHOULD HAVE SEEN THAT COMING.

IT IS DEFINITELY UNWISE TO LET YOURSELF BE DISTRACTED.

YOU SON OF A--

WHICH IS WHY I *DON'T*, OF COURSE.

NNNNAAAH--

THIS BODY WAS GROWN TO BE THE *NEXT* KEEPER--THE SUCCESSOR TO YOUR FRIEND EXETER THERE, WHO'S TRYING *SO* HARD TO STAND UP. A KALIMAWAN MIND-STATE WAS NEVER INSTALLED, SO I DECIDED IT WOULD BE A USEFUL *HOST* FOR THIS *INSTANCE* OF MYSELF...

...I *HAVE* MADE SOME UPGRADES.

NOW, WHY NOT TELL M ABOUT THIS R! IS THAT HARD L TECHNOLOGY? WHAT *POWE SOURCE?* I CO MAKE YOU A *EXCELLENT* D IF YOU WOUL LIKE TO SHARE...

SURE. I'LL SHARE.

YOU *DO* REALIZE THAT I AM MORE THAN CAPABLE OF ABSORBING THAT LEVEL OF ENERGY.

YES. I DO NOT CARE.

YOU ARE *OBSOLETE*, KEEPER. AND YOUR WORLD HAS CHANGED. I'VE MADE IT *MINE*. THERE'S NO PROFIT IN THIS VENTURE FOR YOU.

OR FOR YOU. BECAUSE YOUR "CLIENTS?"

I THINK THEY'D LIKE TO HAVE A WORD. ISN'T THAT RIGHT, ZALLA?

INDEED, KYLE.

IT WASN'T HARD AT ALL. HE SETTLED FOR *QUANTUM* ENCRYPTION ON THE EXOCORTEX INFOSCAPE? HEH. IT WAS NO PROBLEM TO UPLOAD THE ACTUAL DATA ON WHAT THE...ER...WARMONGER WAS DOING.

WHAT HE IS SAYING...

IS THAT THE KALIMAWANS KNOW *EXACTLY* WHAT YOU DID AND BOY, DO THEY LOOK PISSED.

BREAK HIS ARMOR FIRST, GENTLEMEN.

NO! GET OFF ME--

ARE YOU OKAY? ARE *YOU?*

I WASN'T EXPECTING HIM TO BE *QUITE* SO ROIDED UP, BUT I COULD HAVE TAKEN HIM. EVENTUALLY.

YOU SOUND LIKE EXETER.

AND HAL.

GOOD TO KNOW MEN ARE PRETTY MUCH THE SAME EVERYWHERE IN THE UNIVERSE.

WHAT *THOSE* LITTLE BLUE *GHOULS* DID TO MY EQUIPMENT... I...I CAN'T UPLOAD MY CONSCIOUSNESS TO THE FLOW.

KEEPER, THE DECISION BY RIGHTS BELONGS TO YOU.

I DO NOT KNOW WHAT THAT MEANS.

IT MEANS--

I DID NOT SAY I CARED.

I SEE IT NOW. YOU ARE A *COPY.* THE MIND OF A MONSTER, REPLICATED AND BROADCAST. THIS WAS YOUR BACKUP PLAN-- TO SEND YOUR MIND AWAY WHEN DISCOVERED OR DEFEATED.

MY *PRIMARY* WILL WANT REINTEGRATION. I CANNOT ALLOW YOU PRIMITIVES TO RETAIN AN INSTANCE OF MY EXISTENCE. MY PRIMARY *WILL* BE COMING.

YOU ARE A COPY. MEANT TO BE DISPOSABLE. BUT YOU WILL NOT BE DISPOSED OF. YOU WILL MAKE YOURSELF USEFUL.

IF YOU WANT TO MAKE A DEAL, WE CAN--

PLACE HIM IN A SECURE FACILITY.

LOOK, WE CAN TALK ABOUT THIS.

GURK!

THIS IS NOT A NEGOTIATION.

IF HE SPEAKS AGAIN, NAIL HIS TONGUE TO THE NEAREST CONVENIENT SURFACE.

MY WORLD IS...NOT AS I REMEMBER.

THEY DO SAY YOU CAN'T GO HOME AGAIN.

CLEARLY I CAN.

I JUST MEANT--

THAT WAS A JOKE, KYLE RAYNER.

HA. THEN, UH, IT WAS FUNNY...?

CAROL FERRIS WOULD MAKE AN EXCELLENT LIFESHARE.

I DON'T THINK SHE'S DATING AT THE MOMENT, BUT I COULD PROBABLY GET HER NUMBER FOR YOU.

YOU ARE A FOOL, KYLE RAYNER. YOU DO NOT SEE WHAT IS RIGHT BEFORE YOU.

... I DON'T KNOW WHAT YOU'RE TALKING ABOUT.

IT IS NOT IMPORTANT.

OKAY, I'M GOING TO CHANGE THE SUBJECT ENTIRELY BECAUSE THIS IS SUPER AWKWARD. DO YOU NEED US TO STAY, HELP FIX THIS?

NO. YOU CANNOT SOLVE ALL THE PROBLEMS OF OTHERS. THIS WE MUST FIX OURSELVES.

FOR YEARS, I STOOD ALONE, ON THE EDGE OF THE UNIVERSE... BELIEVING I WAS ALONE IN MY RESPONSIBILITY.

I WAS WRONG.

REMEMBER THAT UNTIL WE MEET AGAIN, KYLE RAYNER.